Praise for *Live Courageously*

I first met Vanessa in 2013 on a cold, grey day in Edinburgh, Scotland where we had both been recruited as coaches to support women through a leadership programme. She lit up the room with her warm infectious energy and passion for the work she was called to do. I knew from that first moment I wanted to be in her tribe! Since that day I have been privileged to work alongside this gifted coach and be witness to this woman's own journey of courageous change. If ever there was a role model for walking her talk, then you need to look no further than Vanessa.

Her continued commitment and investment to her own learning and development means in this book we benefit from her expertise and gain understanding at a deeper level the reasons for our struggle.

When we are caught in a cycle of overwhelm and "I am not enough" Vanessa shows us that there is another way and shares practical techniques that she has used with her many clients to help women reclaim their power.

To live courageously is a practice and Vanessa shows us the "how to" with a simple structure that can be easily incorporated into our daily lives. Vanessa shows us that the most important relationship we have in life is the one we have with ourselves.

Over the years Vanessa has been my own coach, teacher and friend and in reading this book she will also be yours.

— **Denise Chilton**, Executive Career and Leadership Coach and Author

This book shines a gentle yet powerful light on the experience of so many women. Vanessa beautifully captures not just her own vulnerable experience of unfolding her past insecurities into living more courageously, but also softly invites her readers to begin their own unfolding so that they can stretch out and powerfully claim the space that their true self takes up. The case studies are highly relatable, and a deep reflection of what many of us see in ourselves. This book is a must-read for any woman who senses they need to shed the skin they're in and re-emerge to own the shape that's stayed hidden within.

— **Christina Hutchinson,** Confidence and Performance Coach and Founder of Mountain High Coaching

A relatable guide and support for all of us women out there. Very readable with easily applicable tools and advice; this is a book that I will certainly go back to in the future, many, many times!

— **Alice Watson-Smith,** Managing Director, Fine & Country, French Riviera

Rediscovering yourself to be able to courageously leave behind that expected, conditioned life is the best gift you could possibly give yourself. That's what this book is all about. A gift to yourself to start living courageously.

Courage is never easy, but rest assured Vanessa won't try to sugar-coat it. Instead, she'll tell you that as hard as it is, it's worth making this choice. She'll keep reminding you that to redefine your identity on your own terms you need no one's permission. To do this most important work of your life and leadership, all you need is to break your own rules so you can become more of who you truly are.

— **Zana Goic Petricevic,** Leadership Coach and Author

A guide to living a brave and authentic life

LIVE
Courageously

VANESSA MAY

Cover image by: ink.Sharia, 99Designs
Book design by: SWATT Books Ltd

Printed in the United Kingdom
First Printing, 2023

ISBN: 978-1-7393136-0-9 (Paperback)
ISBN: 978-1-7393136-1-6 (eBook)

Courage Unfolding Ltd
Leighton Buzzard
LU7 4QQ

www.courageunfolding.com

Contents

———————

Act   **189**

Acknowledgements

This book is the product of all the teachers, coaches, clients, mentors, guides, family and friends that have been with me since the start of my seeking journey. As well as helping me to find my courage, so many of you have been through your own courage process, and these have been sources of so much inspiration in these pages. I am grateful to you all.

Acknowledgements

Foreword

———————————

We live at a time when the need to find ways to ground ourselves, stay focused and draw on our inner strengths has never been greater. A time when understanding how we truly feel and what we really want, have become questions that need answering. And we need a process to help us to answer them – a live courageously process.

As a coach and a woman, I know that the work we do on ourselves is more important than the work we do with or for others. Because when we become the best version of ourselves that we might imagine – happy, emotionally balanced, healthy, and purposeful, we make the greatest contribution to the people around us.

Unfortunately, daily life, with its conformist rituals and routines can easily obstruct our ability to see what it is that we need to do. We become disconnected from the internal navigation systems that help us know that we are in the wrong job, wrong marriage, wrong town, etc. Some part of us knows that we crave change, and yet we are conditioned into a patterned resistance to that, e.g. "Yes, there's stuff I need to deal with, I'm going to get into that self-development thing soon" (but not now). Many of us have no clue as to the untapped powerhouse of emotions within us, where unmet/repressed feelings wait to be noticed, acknowledged, and processed through towards freedom. Down those dark corridors lurks the potential of our soul's liberation and the true beauty of life, and yet instead we choose avoidance and distraction. TV, Netflix, social media, alcohol, food, online shopping – name your poison.

So, how can this book help us to cut through the fog of avoidance and distraction? Live Courageously brings together the objective and structured (the Live Courageously Process) with the subjective (the collection of emotions unique to you). This book also provides the tools to support your journey and find the courage to carve out a plan of action that puts you first. So many women find that idea such a challenge, because of the implications and personal conflicts involved. Vanessa's own journey is bound up in this process, and so is that of many women Vanessa has worked with and helped over the years, and whose voices are heard in this book too.

Courage seems to be in short supply for so many women, so what better time to find ways to unearth this precious commodity in ourselves?

With love and blessings,

Julie Starr, author of The Coaching Manual, The Mentoring Manual, and others.

An introduction to
Live Courageously

Before you step in and claim the life you want to lead, you must learn to get out of overwhelm, navigate through fear, doubt and anxiety to use your courage to live intentionally according to your own terms.

To live courageously is a process in which you feel deeply connected to yourself and your energy systems. You are rooted to your innate worthiness and strengths, aligned to your core values and leadership, and supported as you take action towards what you want.

The opposite of living courageously is living a conditioned life. A life where you lack the internal safety to speak your truth and set your life up according to your own terms. It's a life where you know, understand and comply with the rules set by your family, education, and cultural shaping.

In the conditioned life, you use your sensitivity, empathy and intuition to sense what you need to do to fit in and belong, and shapeshift and adapt yourself accordingly. This becomes so familiar that over time you find yourself disappearing in plain sight. Life and work are safe, predictable and suffocating because you're unconsciously dancing to society's values, beat and rhythm.

But over time there's a cost to you and your relationships at work and at home because a part of you knows you are not being your full and best self.

One of the warning signals that you're living an expected, conditioned life is the feeling that something's missing. You search externally for it but nothing satisfies the itch. Another signal is overwhelm and a feeling of being emotionally flooded. You find yourself constantly pulled in a million directions and need to push hard to keep up with ever increasing to-do lists and demands.

Overwhelm is often suppressed by choosing to resort to habitual patterns of behaviour. Instead of responding to the overwhelm and slowing down, you suppress the anxious feelings and push through regardless. It drives a constant doing mentality and you're always on the go. But what you don't see is that this incessant busyness is an emotional anaesthetic. If unchecked this behaviour leads to role overload, relationship difficulties, resentment and burnout.

Paternalistic societies have conditioned women to believe that it is in our best interests to accommodate, do as we're told, please, conform, be stoic and seek acceptance. As an empath you're ready and able to read the emotional signs in others... perhaps too ready and able. You sense when they're irritated, out of sorts, hurt, isolated or on the edge of rage. You know how to soothe, support and be with them in these moments but if your boundaries are unclear and you're not grounded, you can't distinguish between what's theirs or yours and you get lost in a feeling of confusion and overwhelm.

It feels like you're a boat being blown in different directions, unable to drop your anchor and remind yourself where you are and where you're heading. At work you may find yourself being pushed and pulled by other people's emotions, caught in drama and gossip, not wanting to hurt anyone and taking on everyone else's demands. At home you may find yourself doing everything for everyone in your desire to be a good wife, mother, daughter, sister or friend. In taking on everyone else's agenda and responsibility you cannot hear your own. You can't sense what you feel or need because you're in the noise of everyone else's.

The misguided belief is that by doing all this your needs will be met, you will be safe, belong and prosper. But these behaviours are in fact self-destructive. They create a constant hustle for worthiness and belonging and result in a lack of autonomy, agency and freedom. They make you a victim to your circumstances as opposed to being an owner.

It's unsurprising that you feel helpless to change things because conditioning has supported you to believe this is what to expect: women juggle career, family life and households because it's what they do. Your gifts of intuition, empathy and sensitivity were not taught as part of the curriculum. So, whilst they may have been valued in the playground there was no qualification to validate their importance.

In the world of work the masculine way of working is revered: set goals, create structures, make logical progress towards them and drive results. To get along and move up you have needed to become more focused on that way of working. But in doing so you have marginalised your true gifts of empathy and intuition. If you have felt or expressed emotion, you have been judged as weak. If you have admitted you didn't know or understand something you have been considered less favourably to your colleagues in a compete-and-compare performance ranking system. You have concluded that to get ahead you need to behave more like the men and so you have internalised that marginalisation of your empathy and intuition.

Yet despite the futility and learned helplessness, at the same time you have a deep frustration in this pattern of reactive behaviour of complying, fitting in and protecting yourself. That frustration is a sign that something new wants to manifest itself but your years of conditioning keep preventing you from responding to that feeling, and so you prevent yourself from breaking through.

You're reading this because you want to feel fulfilled, authentic and at peace within yourself. Regardless of your current experience, your age, or your financial situation, you can reclaim your power and align with your authentic knowing. You can reconnect with your own resourcefulness, get beyond the drama and reaction, and take charge of your current circumstances to create more connection, align with your true nature and discover true fulfilment.

Let's break through and transform.

My courage story

I was firmly established in the on/off routine of my life. There were times when I felt strong, confident and capable and others where I doubted and felt like an imposter. There was a rhythm to my life of pushing hard, keeping going, burning out and then needing to disconnect. Sounds familiar?

Home life felt safe in its familiarity but it wasn't fulfilling and was often frustrating. After 22 years of married life, two teenage daughters and a dog, we still argued about the same small things: who had done what or had forgotten to do it or done it wrong. The washing, the in-laws and the lack of money were hot topics in our house. We bickered. We complained. We fought. We made up. We got along. Things felt better and then the fall-outs would all start up again.

Round and around I went. Same cycle, different players. There was a constant underlying feeling of being stuck and longing for change. Life felt beige with moments of colour. Lots of trying hard to improve things. Trying to improve me – to be better. Trying to improve us. Trying to change work. Trying to influence. Trying to persuade. Trying to demonstrate or inspire possibility. Lots of wasted effort. A repetitive cycle of hoping and believing in the possibility of change but observing those hopes being dashed. The pull of equilibrium stronger than the push for change.

I would think, "But it's not that bad is it?" There were lots of things to be grateful for. I was lucky; I could pay my bills and I did have work. We were healthy and happyish. I loved my running and I had friends. Surely I should count my blessings? But somehow this thinking felt like I was tricking myself because a part of me knew I was not built for the merely OK.

Pressure. Confusion. Analysis paralysis. Stuck. Familiarity. Frustration. Growing resentment. Increased self-loathing and sabotaging. It felt like everything was on my shoulders and I felt like it was all my fault. I was taking all the responsibility and yes, it felt deeply personal.

None of my efforts made significant change happen. I tried hard to change me, my husband (so he could help more with the financial pressure, the disciplinarian role, family work and responsibilities), and my work. I was just about keeping it all together, but the cracks were there.

Every fire begins with a spark. Mine was the most shattering of sparks.

"I've been having an affair, is that what you want to hear?" Those were the words that blew everything up. They shook my world view and completely flipped it. Whether it was only an emotional affair or not, it meant that my husband felt closer to someone else. It meant there was secrecy, and it explained all the feelings of disconnection, uninterest, and avoidance. It meant that he was no longer in our marriage and that's why I had those feelings of it all being on my shoulders because it was. Those words hit my body like a punch to the stomach.

That was the real spark and where the transformation began. The ultimate moment of choice, to consider and decide what to do with the state of our marriage. Shit had happened, a core value had been breached, trust had gone, and I was finally awake to it. I had to figure out what to do about it. Who did I need to be – for me, for the family, for the relationship?

I couldn't just go round again in the same way. I couldn't not know what I knew. But there were voices in my head about expectations and what people would think. Whilst the shame and embarrassment that our relationship had broken down had a stranglehold on me, something was different. I couldn't paper over the cracks this time. I couldn't pretend it was all fine when it wasn't. I didn't want to feel like a victim to my circumstances.

I didn't want to act out and gain sympathy for the unfairness of it all. I knew differently. I knew this had happened for a reason and that every relationship has its own intelligence within it and that ours was signalling a big need for change.

I had to choose consciously and with clear intention because it wasn't just me that would be impacted. The impact would ripple. The girls would be hugely affected – hell, even the dog. And I wasn't getting any younger. If I wanted to make a difference it was clear my time was running out.

I tell you this story because I know I am not alone. Through my work I meet women, just like me, who are frustrated, overwhelmed, and stuck. They're intelligent, capable, empathic, intuitive women pulled in a million directions. They juggle work and life, trying to hold on to perfected images of everything being rosy and them having their shit together. They secretly harbour thoughts that somehow what's happening is not fair, it should be different and, deep down, it's not working.

Whilst there is all too often a resigned acceptance to these situations, frustration periodically rears up. So many women feel stressed, anxious, and exhausted keeping up the facades, trying to meet ludicrous expectations and hiding their true emotions. They're fed up being told they're disruptive, difficult, oversensitive or irrational. They're tired of being required to evidence everything before ideas at work can be explored. They're done with staying silent when they hear senior male leaders talk about other women as difficult, emotional, or hormonal. They no longer want to be consigned to being the one taking the notes in every meeting and a thousand other signifiers of being made to feel of less worth.

They want to know if their male counterparts were also told to catch up their hours when they had to home-school and work during the pandemic. They don't want to jump to apologise if something's wrong or not working. They don't want to keep saying the same thing over and over until someone listens and considers their ideas. They don't want to be like the men to get ahead and navigate a man's world.

Despite longing for change they're stuck. This keeping up appearances, pretending that they're superwomen, has taken its toll. Just when they decide to speak up, they get a lump in their throat. A voice in their head directs them to keep quiet and settle. They secretly doubt and think they'll be found out as an imposter, that they don't have their shit together or they can't keep up.

They doubt why they've been given the job – are they the token woman at the table? They wonder if they're too much, not enough, too old, too loud, too quiet… too something. They feel like they've lost some of their confidence and that makes them question if they really do know their own mind and want what they say they want.

These women have one thing in common. They are at an edge of change, wanting something to be different but scared they can't have it. The way they've been shaped by their environment and upbringing is preventing them from creating the shift they long for.

Their culture and conditioning have taught them to be nice, to stay within their box, to know their place, to work hard, to strive to be good, to avoid conflict and settle for less. They've been advised that if something isn't working, don't abandon ship but dig in and try to fix it. This conditioning causes them to sidestep their courage and leaves them at the edge of what they want, doubting and frustrated.

It was the catalyst of my marriage breakdown that helped me to finally take charge and cross the edge of my comfort zone into the dark wood of what was to unfold. It was that choice that led me here to writing this book despite the 15 years of wanting, trying, and failing to write it previously.

The difference is that in writing this, I am honouring a commitment to myself and to all the overwhelmed women, struggling to keep everything in place, hoping for change whilst clinging to safety and conditioning. And, as well as telling you about my experiences, this book is full of many other voices. Women, with their own doubts and struggles, encountering their own moments of change and courage. There are inspiring case studies in every chapter from women from all walks of life, so that, if my specific circumstances and journey don't chime with your own inner struggles, I am sure some of those voices will.

There is another way.

Whatever your spark, whether it's a marriage breakdown, a decision not to be silenced, a feeling of burnout, a fear of regret, a glass ceiling, or a yearning to rise, you can navigate through the turbulence and discover your courageous and authentic self.

Sometimes you need permission to change. My permission came in that moment when my husband said those words. I had this breathtaking moment of calm and the only voice in my head was Maya Angelou's: "Love liberates".[1]

It was time to liberate both of us from this dysfunctional situation. But who the hell was I? I finally accepted that I couldn't change the person I'd spent 32 years of my life with and that it wasn't my job to do that either. He was fine just the way he was, and I was too, but the question of our compatibility was (and always had been) the real issue.

It's fair to say that despite 20-plus years in personal development and coaching I was at a point where I didn't recognise myself. I had shapeshifted myself to adapt to my relationships. It sounds crazy but it's true. Physician, heal thyself! You see, when you want to be liked and loved you will do things unconsciously to create that outcome. Now I had to rediscover myself all over again.

But where should I begin? Surely I was someone that should know better, be better and do better? I had access to all this knowledge through my work but as we all know, wisdom is only gained through its application.

So, as I stood on the edge of an ending, full of overwhelming emotions, surrounded by people who were labouring on in their marriages and careers, I trusted my instinct and took the plunge into the unknown.

I thought to myself that had I predicted this sudden life-changing event I probably wouldn't have made the decision to quit my corporate job at the start of that year and build my coaching business. I would have established a savings and pensions plan. I would have been prepared.

The funny thing was, in retrospect I was prepared. My training had prepared me. I knew how to lead myself. I knew how to take a stance for something. I knew how to navigate through difficult emotions. I had just never had to apply it in quite such a personal and painful way.

My goals were clear:

1. A good divorce where we remain amicable
2. For myself, our girls, the dog and my ex-husband to be OK
3. A fair and reasonable split
4. A prospering coaching business that makes a difference and contributes to women claiming their power and authority

Sounds simple, doesn't it, but I had to upgrade my internal operating system, stop waiting for someone to rescue me and step into growing up again. I had to use my empathy and intuition to navigate through the dark wood instead of adapting to make everyone else happy. I had to empower myself to be courageous, to stop thinking I was unkind for speaking my truth and standing up for my needs and let go of worrying about what would happen to the girls and my husband on the other side of this change… I had to create clear boundaries. I trusted that they were resourceful, creative and whole and that with transparency and clarity we would create a new normal. I leant into the knowing that clarity is kindness.

At 51 I was discovering my adulthood and redefining my identity.

In the next 12 months, I chose to do the following:

- End my marriage
- Accept that I had lost trust in my own feelings, emotions, and needs
- Learn to advocate for myself, to connect to myself

- Claim my feminine and masculine power, take charge, and stand by myself
- Liberate my nature, authenticity and spirit, and discover my true leadership

It wasn't that I felt invincible. I didn't. I felt terrified, every single step of the way. I still do. There are many days and nights when I ask myself what I have done and question if I did the right thing. But I recognise all this for what it is: nostalgia for life before the disruptive spark.

I realised that I had to stop caring about what people thought and letting the unconscious goal of fitting in and being liked rule me. I chose to release the internal pressure to be good, to push, to strive as if I was still in school pushing for some kind of invisible unattainable A grade: the good mother, great wife, great contributor and overall nice, decent human being award.

I chose to redesign my life on my own terms. I hired a worthiness coach, a book mentor, and a counsellor, to support me. I ignored the stories that I had about how I couldn't afford it and I chose to invest in myself. I peeled away layers of my inner conditioning, I questioned, I cried, I laughed, and I worked hard to challenge myself. I leant into conflict instead of away from it and I used my values to navigate me through.

Ultimately, I had to find a new version of myself. A more honest, truer, soulful Vanessa. I had to learn to advocate for myself, particularly as my health and financial challenges kicked in.

I have learnt that living courageously requires you to deeply know and accept yourself. You cannot do it without honouring and loving your true self. You must take all the parts of you, your mind, body, spirit and emotions, and communicate with all of them and not let one part dominate.

You must learn the skills to master these different aspects of you and create a practice that brings you into wholeness. Courage and sovereignty go together with self-acceptance and love, not for the who you should become but for the who you naturally are. This deep acceptance and acknowledgement empower you to set your life up by design.

Being a sensitive, intuitive empath in a world of logic and results is challenging. I was not taught how to manage my gifts. Firstly, I can lose myself in other people. I feel their pain deeply. It unconsciously attracts my desire to help and heal, but in doing so, I can abandon myself in favour of someone else. This makes it hard to remember and prioritise myself because my life becomes 'other' focused.

Secondly, I see the potential in others. I see a bigger picture than is presented to me and fall in love with possibility. I champion and encourage that possibility to be realised in the other person but lose sight of the fact that the other person's agenda may not be to fulfil the potential I see. As a result, I lose my energy and self in others.

My journey has involved learning the skills and practices that I wasn't taught. I have amazing parents who are kind, generous and deeply caring. But they, like me, cannot teach what they don't have.

There was no clear path to embracing my gifts of being an intuitive thinker and sensitive feeler. I had to accept the self-inflicted pain of self-judgement and the isolation that creates. Most importantly, I had to learn how to rule my world whilst embracing the diversity and differences of others.

I had lost myself in my marriage and work, and in the limiting beliefs that I held unconsciously within me. The effort to find myself has taken me down many paths but realising that the wisdom was inside me was key. I had to dig deep and discover my sovereignty, set my life up by design, and unleash my gifts to fully support my newly discovered self.

What have been the key discoveries I've made for myself and for women at a similar moment of change?

- I CAN choose when and where to take up space in the world, and how much

- Advocating for yourself requires knowing what you feel and what it is that you need
- Be an observer of yourself, not a reactor, so that you can create time and space to act out of choice
- Be careful what you track evidence for (don't worry, you'll find it!)
- People who care about you know who you are
- Feeling valued and treasured starts within you
- We are all worthy of being comforted and supported
- It IS possible, at any age, to build a new tribe of emotionally available and intuitively responsive friends
- Determine who gives you a feeling of safety… like melted butter!
- Your inner authority should always win versus your inner apology
- Know that you are worthy of attention
- We are all free to be messy and imperfect
- If someone is uncomfortable it doesn't have to be you
- There is no need to be a barometer for other people's moods
- Allow yourself to be with people who have the capacity to be with you without trying to change or fix you
- Give yourself permission to play and be at ease

It's not just you

Every client I have ever worked with has got caught at the edge of change, waiting for permission, courage, or some sign to tell them that it is the right move. They want to know they will be safe and hunger for predictability and security.

No one externally can tell you if it's the right move, but you can be aware of the choice points and learn to listen to yourself. You can learn to trust yourself and discern what intuitively feels aligned. You can rediscover your sovereignty at any stage of your life – even at 51! You can find the courage to set your work and life up on your own terms.

In 2017 I was working as an executive coach and was gathering video testimonials for a leadership development programme I had designed and run. Well, I call it a leadership development programme but actually it was helping senior leaders in the tech industry to build relationships and enhance their people management skills.

They wanted to have real conversations, build connection, and manage their emotions so that they could perform at their best. I covered topics like courageous conversations, creating your own luck, building resilience, and influencing.

One of the participants said the following, "We are not taught these skills at university. They're life skills. I don't understand why. Everyone should know this." I noted this information and unconsciously pushed it to the back of my mind.

I'd been aware for a while that there was a problem, but I couldn't clearly define it. Since going through my own personal experience in 2019, there has been a shift in the clients that I am working with. I have found myself working with women who want to lead. The more women I meet and whose stories I hear, the more I realise that the question I had asked myself, "Is it just me?", is a universal question.

I had never anticipated working primarily with women, because my early experience of girls was not pleasant. There was a hustling and competitiveness at school that I didn't enjoy. I saw this repeated in the workplace, where women were striving to get ahead and hustling for success. They had no qualms at throwing each under the bus to get ahead. Some were far more subtle in their behaviours and used control, needing to be at every meeting or fake niceness and then gossip to manipulate and curry favour. It was as if only one person could win at climbing the ladder. You were either a bitch or a doormat.

Women were showing up to coaching and sharing their frustrations, their sadness, their hopes for a different way of working and living but also their fears that it wasn't possible. These women were lost in the middle of that process, either on the edge of burnout feeling overwhelmed because it wasn't possible to deliver on work and life expectations or lost in the myth that they had held for how they thought it was all going to end up. But the biggest loss they were facing was of their true nature. Many women described feeling like an imposter.

These women had shared anxieties about being not enough, too much, too late, too young, too old. They all had some internal clock that ticked along, creating both a sense of urgency and of frustration. They all made comparisons to other women that they didn't necessarily know but assumed were doing better or were further ahead than they were. They connected to their worth with external achievements and the validation that arose from that. As a consequence, they were pushing hard but never really feeling that sense of freedom and congruence that comes from knowing and accepting who you are and what you're here to do.

I realised that my purpose was to connect women back to their essence and courage and share stories that helped them to choose consciously and live well according to their terms.

My research

To validate my thoughts, I conducted a survey in January 2022 as part of the research for this book. I reached out to women juggling the work and life balance.

I wanted to know what was going on with them, what their struggles were and what they longed for. Having coached career women in various leadership roles, I was already aware of this constant pressure and challenge in navigating work and life and the patriarchy that is still ever present in our working worlds. I wanted to know how I could really serve these women to become more of their courageous selves and sharpen my own focus in my work to better serve them.

The headline results as to how these women were spending their time were that:

- 72% of working women reported they are plate-spinning all the time
- 60% said they felt it was easier and better to do the job themselves than get help from others and
- 52% described themselves as the go-to person for everything.

Interestingly, over half of these plate-spinning, capable women described feeling that they were not doing well at any one thing, compared themselves frequently to others and had a desire to be liked. There was a strong sense of frustration running through these results.

When you live and work in a society that has you feeling like you're failing if you can't do and be all that you think you should, you compare yourself to others who are hiding behind their own defences of perceived perfectionism but you have no idea if the person you are comparing yourself to really has it all together or not.

So, despite the plethora of self-help books advising how you should treat yourself differently, women are still resorting to comparison. Clearly, advising women to be kinder, more loving, and self-compassionate isn't working.

How do I know? In my research 93% of these women described themselves as being self-critical. These are smart, intelligent women juggling their careers and lives. They are plate-spinning all the time and giving themselves an incredibly hard time in the process. It's hard to make progress when you're beating yourself up constantly. It's like putting your foot on the accelerator whilst also having the handbrake on. Yet they continue in this fashion, that is until they wake up to the whole cycle and explore what's underneath the constant busyness and striving.

What is courage?

I'm not going to sugar-coat this because it won't serve you. Courage is hard. Taking courageous action is never easy until you're on the other side of it.

It takes courage for women to stand in a new way of being and doing when they've been conditioned to be good, do the right thing and strive to discover their happy-ever-after. It's hard to be yourself when you've been manipulated to think that you're too much, not enough and should constantly push to do and be better than you naturally already are.

Courage means knowing and accepting yourself as you are and finding a way to take consistent action towards what deeply matters to you. You need to stop suppressing your emotions and avoiding telling people what's really going on and ask for what you need. You must tune out the noise, other people's opinion, your desire to be liked and loved, and get completely behind yourself.

You must find psychological safety within yourself and not make it conditional on others' wellbeing or love and acceptance. It means accepting and embracing your thoughts and feelings and finding a way for them to work in harmony together instead of derailing you in paralysis analysis or overwhelm.

Let's think about some of the everyday ways courage shows up for working women:

- Navigating the constant voice in your head that doesn't shut up and leaves you doubting, guilty and overthinking
- Saying no in its many guises, including to being the notetaker in meetings because "you're so good at it"
- Dealing with the aftermath when you speak your truth and others disagree or retaliate
- Declining the next project because not doing it might be career limiting even though you can prove it's not achievable anyway
- Getting a divorce or ending a relationship when it's easier not to

- Asking to be paid on equal terms when you know you deserve it
- Refusing to play toxic games with those around you and stepping out of the drama
- Using your guilt to put in healthy boundaries instead of putting yourself down
- Refusing to be run by a presenteeism culture that keeps you overworked and dissatisfied
- Working with colleagues in the workplace who go out of their way to try and put you down despite the quality and quantity of your work
- Refusing to people-please and choosing to assert your needs
- Being at the pinnacle of your career knowing your hormones are wreaking havoc and being able to talk about it, own it and not allow it to undermine your confidence or authority

Underneath courage is a commitment to being yourself, backing yourself and your leadership. But women can direct their efforts to be perfect rather than show up as they are. I consciously chose to use 'hard' to describe courage because in life today we are impatient for immediate results and can have an expectation that it should come easily. Just as it takes time and careful pruning to cultivate and grow a bonsai tree, it takes time to make deep and sustainable changes. If you've had a lifetime of subjugating yourself or putting others first, it will take time, practice and reinforcement to change this.

My clients describe feeling torn and pulled in a million directions in so many ways. Typical ones include:

- Living someone else's dreams/values/life
- Trying to get it right, but it's someone else's blueprint
- Unable to end what's unhealthy for them
- Trying to attain perfection and achieve balance
- Making other opinions matter more than their own
- Unable to let go of control and empower others
- Sweating the small stuff
- Overwhelmed by emotion

- Confused by different voices / parts of their self saying different things
- In transition and not knowing what's next
- Unable to act towards goals
- Forgotten who they are and what they want

Rarely do women stop to pause and ask, is what I want really what I need? What do I want? Rarely do we ask, is the way I'm working correct for me?

Courage demands you know what you want and empower yourself. It therefore requires you to live consciously and make choices according to your own definitions and measures of success. So, for me courage and conscious living go hand in hand.

Let's explore what these women said they really wanted.

63% wanted to feel confident in telling someone when a line has been crossed.

56% wanted to feel more confident and to experience less doubt.

51% wanted to be able to ask for help without feeling weak.

What they didn't say was that they wanted a bigger house, a better car, a different wardrobe, or even more holidays. Yet this is often part of the myth that you're caught up in. Your pain points are constantly marketed to, highlighting the need for you to be and do better. This is what sells lifestyles and products.

Having worked with hundreds of coaching clients over the years, these reports of chasing and hustling are all too familiar. Whilst you may have been conditioned to think the answer lies outside of you, it doesn't. It lies deep within because if you're doing this behaviour in reaction to something then you must also have the solution inside you.

"I don't ever put myself first"
"I often say yes to things which I later get upset about"

"I have no energy left for me"

"I don't charge what I'm worth; perhaps others don't value me"

"I am afraid to let others down"

"I can't seem to back myself without needing external validation"

"I feel like I have nothing to offer and can't get things right"

This is just a sample of what women have been telling me.

There is another way

I wrote this book because I want you to know that there is another way.

Wisdom is earned, intellect is studied. If you are seeking knowledge and information outside of you but not applying it, you are in a pattern of constant seeking but never finding. You think if you just learn more and keep going you will get to the other side. But the thing is, you won't, and if there was a school report at the end of your life that read *tries hard but,* you'd probably feel deeply disappointed.

The feeling of overwhelm and self-doubt can be changed. If you feel lost, you are still there waiting to be found. You do not have to stay in this repeating cycle.

This book won't help you to find a miracle way to be even more productive. It will help you to give yourself a different kind of award and acknowledgement. Instead of trying to achieve an 'A' in everything you do, you are going to accept where you are, audit your work and life set-up, and choose a different kind of adventure and courageous action.

It's through this process that you will rediscover your aliveness and authenticity and choose if you're willing to take a stance for yourself. This will be as a result of accepting that you have unique gifts and expression, and that these deserve to be seen and heard.

This book is a sharing of stories of working women: mine and others. I wrote this book because I want you to recognise those difficult places, so you no longer hide in the shadows, thinking you're the only one trying relentlessly to keep up appearances.

The first intention behind the book is to lift the veil of secrecy that many of us hide behind so that we can have real conversations about what it means to be a woman in the workplace, have healthy striving and lead a life well-lived.

The second intention is to give you a process that you can work through, so that you can reflect on your journey and find the courage to take charge of what you really want but right now are scared to have.

At the heart of being courageous is living consciously.

I believe that you really are innately worthy as a human being, just as you are, born now with a unique purpose and incredible strengths. No one else can express your strengths the way you can. Ignore them and the world loses them.

This book will help you understand the deeper reason behind your feelings of doubt and burnout. It will wake you up to the choice you face, to stand and advocate for your true nature and let go of the hustle to belong and be worthy.

It will offer you a framework to help you remember who you are and what makes you unique. Whether like me you're transitioning from divorce, you want to take yourself seriously and to the next level, or you simply want to feel better, this practical process will help you unlock your own wisdom and develop practices to drop the hustle, redefine success and live according to your terms.

If you want to take the push and strain out of it all and you know that you're working too hard but it's taking you further away from your true self, you can choose to empower yourself.

There are 3 simple underlying principles to this book:

1. It is your life – you choose how you do and be in it. You decide to bring your gifts to it.
2. You define the terms of what it means to live well and create success on your own terms.
3. You are responsible for staying in your own state of ease.

What I have learnt is true in mine and in my clients' journeys is that you must go through a messy, unknown part to break through and discover something new on the other side of the learning journey. You don't come out the same. And it's that decision to end a chapter, be in the messy middle of the unknown and begin a new beginning, that changes who you know yourself to be.

It starts with awareness, accepting reality and making a conscious decision to shift. You don't just need to change your mindset or emotions; you must also decide to take up space for yourself and commit to doing something different.

This is about returning to your wholeness and navigating this crazy world with grace and confidence. In this book I will take you through a simple, memorable process to give you agency and achieve balance, fulfilment, and ease. I call this the Live Courageously Process and it follows 5 stages:

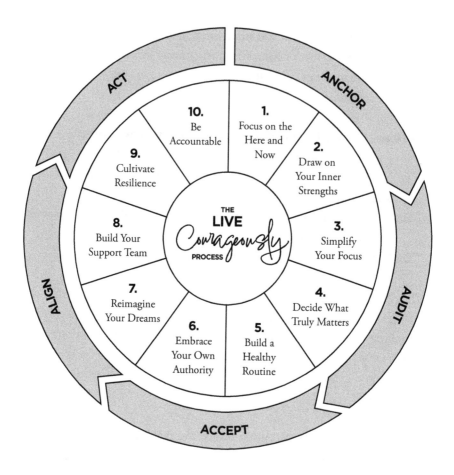

Anchor

1. Focus on the here and now

When you feel overwhelmed, anxiety drives overthinking, avoidance, and procrastination. You get caught worrying about the future or being lost ruminating in the past. So, I explore a **Slow Down, Pause and Breathe** courage practice to help you ground that negative spiralling 'what if' energy. You will learn a simple method to break your own self-limiting pattern, get out of your head and reset. With practice you will learn to recover your grounding and sense of inner calm and ease.

2. Draw on your inner strengths

When life is stuffed with unrealistically high expectations and constant doing, you can lose sight of your strengths and resourcefulness in the drive to meet them. I share with you a **Build Core Strength** courage practice to reconnect to your knowledge, skills, experience and self-belief, to guide you in the moment.

Audit

3. Simplify your focus

When your head is full you can't focus clearly. Completing a **Be Intentional** courage audit will help you discern what's driving you and what to prioritise to create meaningful change. Choosing consciously where to put the focus of your attention is the essence of this courage practice.

4. Decide what truly matters

Our world is noisy, with constant subliminal messaging that pushes our behaviour towards consumerism and markets to our insecurities. The courage practice **Live Your Values** will support you to reclarify and prioritise what matters to you.

Accept

5. Build a healthy routine

The myth that women make better multi-taskers is just that, a myth, as there is no clear evidence for it. It is one that has been conveniently set up by the world to set you up for unhealthy striving, trying to do and have it all. Learning to define your own routine will support you in your journey towards living your authentic life. The courage practice **Set Your Own Rhythm** will support you to take back control and know what fulfilment is for you.

6. Embrace your own authority

You are not an apology – you are an authority in yourself, what you like, how you want to set your work and life up to support you and your relationships. The courage practice to **Rule Your World** will give you agency and permission to approve of yourself and rise in your own life and work.

Align

7. Reimagine your dreams

When you've lost faith, your heart feels broken and the vulnerability of knowing that you might never realise your dreams feels too great, and so you can lose yourself to your disappointments. The courage practice **Dare to Dream** will support you in rediscovering your own dreaming again.

8. Build your support team

Everyone at some point in their life needs lifting. As women we have been conditioned to be stoic, strong, independent and capable but the truth is, together is better. So, to help you lean into the right people without losing yourself or your resourcefulness, I've created the **Define Your Support Team** courage practice.

Act

9. Cultivate resilience

Cultivating resilience involves the ability to manage your energy to withstand drains and renew it in a way that supports you. It therefore requires you to know that you are innately worthy so that you can create the healthy boundaries needed to enable you to establish limits so that you can focus and conserve your precious energy and attention. Resilience enables you to keep going and see setbacks as temporary whilst continuing the pursuit of your desired vision. So, the **Build Personal Resilience** courage practice will help you, compassionately and resourcefully, to move through any setbacks.

10. Be accountable

Critical to the impetus to act is accountability, and so being accountable is the final element in the courage process. You are much more likely to do what you say if you are accountable, to yourself and to others. In turn, accountability bolsters the power of your support team, as they should be accountable too, along with all the other key players in your professional and personal realms. None of this is about blame – it's about taking responsibility and being clear on where the boundaries lie of what you can influence in any given situation. Accountability and authenticity are linked – each reinforces the other, as the courage practice **Be Accountable and Authentic** demonstrates.

It's your choice

Ultimately this book will encourage you to move out of the repetitive cycle of being stuck, and help you to choose. It's been said that when you don't decide, you decide. It sounds crazy but there's truth in it. When you decide not to decide that is a decision to stay in your current circumstances.

The Live Courageously Process will repeatedly invite you to get conscious and choose. Your history and conditioning may have dictated your life so far, but it doesn't have to be your legacy. The family you were born into, the culture you grew up in, the role you played in the family, that doesn't disappear when you hit adulthood. It is carried with you unconsciously until you slow down and decide to consciously explore it.

Being conscious requires you to slow down your automatic, habitual shortcuts and question. A shortcut is an automatic response that you make without thinking. For example someone asks you to do something, and you automatically say yes. This decision to undertake reflection and analysis is courageous. It's uncomfortable to recognise where you're operating unconsciously merely from habit. But with awareness the choice to liberate arrives. It gives you the opportunity to see and audit your life and behaviours and see whether they support the vision you hold for yourself or are only serving someone else's dream.

Part of being conscious is a commitment to living in the present moment, but human nature and the emotions you feel can pull you back to the past or forward to the future. By auditing where you are now and accepting both your dreams and your reality, you get the choice to align and take courageous action so that you move forward with intention.

This book is designed to be simple, clear and pragmatic. I know you're already experiencing overwhelm so the last thing you need are more 'to do's' to add onto your already long list. Imagine if you were drowning; it wouldn't help to have someone explain what was going on and why it was happening. You would want someone to throw you a lifeline or tell you what to do to save yourself.

Stop saying sorry

You are not an apology. Are you someone that says sorry all the time? Someone bumps into you or crosses your path and the first thing out of your mouth is "Sorry". The meeting at work is heated and you want to share a different perspective, so you say, "Sorry to interrupt" or "Sorry to throw a curveball here." Someone gives you unsolicited feedback and you say, "Sorry you feel that way, it wasn't my intention."

If sorry is a phrase that crosses your lips without awareness, it's time to notice how frequently you say it. When do you apologise and for what? It's hard to hear and accept that you show up with apology. You think you're being polite, respectful and considerate but it's a lie.

The truth is you have opinions and clear points of view. The truth is you're scared that others will think you're stupid, that the tribe will make you an outcast and you will be ridiculed, embarrassed and ostracised. But being apologetic means you are not claiming your place in the world. Your apology is a weapon against yourself and your own life. Nature makes no apology. It blossoms and blooms and stands tall because that is what it does naturally in a conducive environment. It can't not be itself.

You deserve a happy, fulfilled life

This doesn't mean that there won't be hard times when you struggle. It does mean that you get to be you and do you – the best way you know how. You don't have to push to be in someone else's lane or version of happiness.

You are not meant to shrink for the sake of safety. You are neither too much nor not enough, but you are likely to have a habit of thinking these thoughts. It is your birthright to take up space, be yourself and live your life and purpose your way.

Recognise that it's now your turn.

This book will invite you to stand fully in your innate worthiness and power. It will help you to define success on your own terms and make it your job to hold yourself accountable to your own standards and actions.

It's time to break your own rules

I will show you why and how to do that.

The women I surveyed were not new to personal growth work. 56% had read self-books, 55% had received coaching and 43% had received therapy.

You create change by becoming more of who you are. And that's what we're going to do together through the practices in this book.

By reading and applying the strategies in this book, you will:

- Make a conscious choice and commitment to change (if you choose)
- Discern exactly what needs to change and choose your priorities
- Develop new strategies to feel good inside and take actions that are aligned with your true vision
- Practise, review, learn and build resilience

How to read this book

So, first things first. I want to make it clear, you are not broken, and this book is not here to save you. You are a capable, whole, and creative human being and I respect that in you. You may have thoughts that you're failing, you can't keep up and that somehow, you've got it all wrong, but these thoughts can be changed because you are the one creating them. You may have feelings of sadness, frustration and overwhelm but those feelings do not have to run you; you can learn to ride them like waves.

The book is divided into the five stages of the Live Courageously Process, with each stage covered over two chapters.

1. **Anchor** – focus on the here and now, draw on your inner strengths
2. **Audit** – simplify your focus, decide what truly matters
3. **Accept** – build a healthy routine, embrace your inner authority
4. **Align** – reimagine your dreams, build your support team
5. **Act** – cultivate resilience, be accountable

Each chapter follows a simple format. A few concepts, a story, a simple courage practice and ways to make this work. Each story, laid out as a case study, explores a different form of push or pull. They are stories that have been developed and created from real life but adapted, and names have been changed to maintain confidentiality. With some of the case studies, to illustrate issues and solutions as clearly as possible, some situations are an amalgam of more than one client's experiences. This device, as I hope you will understand, allows me to protect the anonymity of my clients' experiences and the confidences shared during the coaching process.

However, and this is important, this does not detract from the veracity of the experiences I am sharing in these pages. All the issues raised, and ways in which I have worked with my clients to help them, have all taken place, just not maybe in the way that the case studies portray them.

Often my clients have a very different starting point depending on their catalyst. I highlight the parts that are most relevant to each stage in the process so that it is easy to relate each story to the relevant courage practice. There are a variety of tools that I draw on and my intention is to show how they work in practice through the stories. Most clients have gone through the whole process that I share in the book.

The book is designed to guide your thinking. A significant element to the book is that it is designed to be interactive, to become your courage practice diary. There are self-assessment tools for you to fill in, both at the point when you first read it, and importantly, an opportunity to revisit and re-evaluate in, say, one year's time. Don't be afraid to write in this book! It's now your book not mine! Perhaps growing up you, like me, had to cover your schoolbooks to protect them and that created an unconscious psychological barrier to writing inside them. Give yourself permission to use this book as you would a journal. It is designed to support you to write down your inner thoughts, so overcome any resistance to write in it and please use it as intended.

What I ask is that you commit to the practices not as if they are dogma that you must follow, but a bit like a smorgasbord. Try things out and see what works. Take what works and practise it regularly because in fact we're always practising something, and the key is to be conscious about choosing what we practise. If you practise self-criticism, you're going to become masterful at it. The same is true for self-validation and compassion.

You are doing the best you can right now with the tools you have. I'm going to give you a new toolkit and fresh practices that you can try. But the key is the medicine inside you. The tools will help you access your own medicine and learn to become more of your beautiful, brilliant self.

I am a firm believer in intuition, and I want you to trust yours in how you read this book. Sometimes you can pick up a book and it opens at a page that seems to offer you exactly what you are looking for. Why not try that serendipity now and flick open some pages further on in this book?

The main principle that I want you to adopt is that there is no trying without doing. You are reading this because you want a change. I invite you to be willing to have a new experience, reflect on it, try it out and then learn from it.

If you choose to continue with this book, you will at best helicopter above your overwhelm, observe your role in creating it, gain insight into what is driving that and develop new ways to be with yourself so that you can have more calm, balance and fulfilment.

At worst you will read it, put it down and move on to the next book or training course. But I'm guessing you've had enough of that, and in turning to the next chapter you are making a commitment to yourself that you matter and it's time to do you, your work and life a little differently.

Anchor

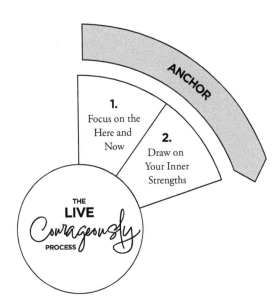

Focus on the here and now

FIND PRESENCE IN OVERWHELM

When you feel overwhelmed, anxiety drives overthinking, avoidance and procrastination. You get caught worrying about the future or being lost ruminating in the past. So, I explore a **Slow Down, Pause and Breathe** *courage practice to help you ground that negative spiralling 'What if' energy. You will learn a simple method to break your own self-limiting pattern, get out of your head and reset. With practice you will learn to recover your grounding and sense of inner calm and ease.*

The Live Courageously Process begins with anchoring in the here and now to enable you to stop reacting, but instead connect to yourself so that you can identify what capacity you have and what you need. This will help you break the cycle of running on empty and saying yes as an automatic, unconscious reaction.

Burnout – the myths that feed it

1. "If I push through it will be fine"

Burnout happens when your capacity to handle things is destroyed. The challenge with stressors is that it's the small unnoticed ones that have a cumulative effect. You think you can handle each individual stressor because it seems insignificant on its own but as the incidents increase your capacity reduces.

A commonly held misguided belief that drives overwhelm is that if you just push through, you'll be fine. You fear that if you stop or slow down it will be perceived as a failure to cope. But pushing through is not an effective strategy when you're overwhelmed. Grit is wonderful when you have a clear goal and want to focus your energy and attention, but if you're already running on empty, reacting to everyone else's needs will drain your already limited energy and your efforts will be inefficient and unproductive.

2. "I'm supposed to be good at multi-tasking because I'm a woman"

Multi-tasking involves doing more than one thing at a time. It requires switching attention between tasks and increases cognitive demand. Multi-tasking has traditionally been perceived as a woman's domain, where she juggles career, running a household and family life.

Studies show that women's brains are no more efficient than men's at switching tasks and juggling multiple tasks at the same time.

This myth sets you up to fail, adds fuel to the fire and feeds the belief that you must somehow be falling short if you can't juggle and keep up. Because you've been told you're supposed to be good at multi-tasking, you're open to manipulation to take on more than you have capacity for. Whilst you may have a strength in optimising and organising your time, you do not have a biological advantage in being able to multi-task.

3. "Everyone else is doing better than me"

When you're in a tight spot it's common to look at others and compare yourself less favourably. The challenge with this behaviour is that it's isolating. It drives disconnection and has you lacking empathy towards yourself.

Unchecked comparisons will feed fear and envy, and drive conflict within yourself and with others. It is not about everyone else. It's about you, your capacity, your desires, your true nature and what it wants to express.

4. "I should be further ahead than where I am"

This myth drives the notion that there is a set place and time where you should be in your work and life. Women are still raised with traditional narratives about expectations on how their life should ideally unfold.

In a world full of push notifications, perfected images and idealised visions, you can think that you're behind everyone else and this creates a false sense of urgency and rush. It creates an undertone of anxiety and drives busyness, over-thinking and can also create procrastination through a desire to get it right. But according to whose version of right?

Start where you are

When you're in overwhelm it feels counterintuitive to stop, pause and reconnect to your breath. Who will do everything if you don't? Your overwhelm may feel such a familiar feeling that you've got used to it and convinced yourself that you can just push through to the other side. But there's a cost to your relationship to yourself and others and eventually the build-up will lead to burnout, resentment, and a need to completely disconnect.

Overwhelm is not fertile ground for effective, clear thinking. It creates constant anxiety, a feeling of being emotionally flooded and a desire to check out. To manage overwhelm and avoid burnout requires you to know and define your own capacity. When your head is full of things to do and worries to think about, it's all too tempting to ignore the need for rest and renewal. You need to connect with yourself and increase your self-awareness.

One way in which you can check in with yourself and create awareness of your current situation is to decide what best describes you right now from the list list below.

1. **BURNT OUT** – exhausted, energy depleted

2. **OVERWHELMED** – unhealthy striving/pushing, being cynical, helplessness

3. **SATISFIED** – healthy striving/flow, balance, fulfillment

4. **UNDERWHELMED** – unfulfilled, bored, apathetic

You cannot change what you cannot see or feel

Humans are masters of self-deception. When you disconnect from your emotions and senses you become preoccupied with your thoughts and find yourself living from the shoulders up. It's vulnerable to choose to connect with the tender parts of you. You may fear that you will be perceived as weak, not coping or somehow less capable than others.

You may use a mask of stoicism or perfection to hide your struggle. You push uncomfortable feelings down and pretend everything is fine, telling yourself that you will do some self-care once you've conquered the to-do list. But lists have a sneaky way of constantly growing and this creates a feeling of constant pressure and chasing to keep up.

Pay attention to the sensations in your body over your thoughts

The mind will lie to you. It will tell you that if you just complete the ten things on your list everything will be better, but this is a recipe for over-functioning, constant busyness and a lack of fulfilment.

On the other hand, your body will not lie. Tension in your shoulders and jaw, teeth grinding, headaches, hot flushes, redness in your face and shortness of breath are all signals that your body is experiencing stress.

Conscious breathing is an opportunity to find presence in the moment, check in with yourself and notice how you're doing. You focus on your breathing and notice the thoughts that come into your head without letting them hook your attention. It takes practice and for those that are addicted to doing, the temptation will be to go and grab a notebook or act on all that thinking but the art is to stay present and focused on the breath.

Connect to your courage to take charge and simply breathe

Breathing is an automatic function controlled through the autonomic nervous system. It is not necessary to think consciously about it, it just happens. But are you aware if you have a poor breathing pattern and the impact of this on your performance and choices?

Your breath continuously rises and falls, but under pressure, when life is challenging, you may unconsciously stop its natural flow. Breathing high up in your chest tightens your muscles and reduces the length of your exhale. It arouses your sympathetic nervous system which is the network of nerves that prepares you for fight or flight.

Slowing down your breath anchors you to the present moment. It grounds your energy. It activates your parasympathetic nervous system (also known as rest and digest) which decreases your heart rate and signals to your body that everything is calm and ok. It's from this place that you will be able to focus, think clearly and do your best performance work.

Become aware of your emotional journey

Overwhelm can simultaneously feel like you're living under a huge rock whilst also being in a cloud of constant confusion. There's high stress, emotions, and a need to think clearly but you just can't. It's often accompanied by this huge sense of pressure, rush, and a feeling that you just can't keep abreast or catch up.

In this place it's hard to understand your emotions. You feel them deeply but don't understand them. Once you calm your nervous system and get present, you are in a better place to explore what's really going on with your emotions and gain insight from them.

Labelling your emotions requires emotional literacy. It's an assumption that adults have this literacy and ability to name their emotions accurately. When you've spent a lifetime fulfilling other people's needs, knowing your own can be deeply challenging.

At the simplest level you have four needs to feel safe within yourself: physical needs, security needs, belonging needs and fulfilment needs. When you operate on automatic pilot, focusing on everyone else, you don't slow down enough to check in with yourself and consider your own needs. However, your energy and emotions will guide you to what you need. They contain packets of information that hold wisdom within them but if you push through or repress them and instead listen to all the 'shoulds' in your head, you will miss the signals to connect to your own authentic needs.

The emotional zones overleaf can help you pinpoint and connect to your feelings and reflect on your needs. From this place you can map your daily, weekly and monthly emotional journey and start to make connections between what you feel and what you need.

I feel...   I need...

**OVERWHELM
PANIC
FRUSTRATION
ANXIOUS
ANNOYED
IRRITATED
BETRAYED**

Space to pause, take a breath, get present
Expression to say what I feel,
get clear on what matters
Autonomy to choose my path,
make my own decisions

**SAD
BORED
DISAPPOINTED
DEPRESSED
ASHAMED
LONELY
TIRED**

Validation, self worth, acceptance,
acknowledgement
Fulfilment to reconnect to my values
and authenticity
Connection, reassurance and compassion
– this too shall pass

**EXCITED
HAPPY
CONFIDENT
BRAVE
EMPOWERED
PASSIONATE
LOVING**

Celebrate and acknowledge
what's working
Appreciate what I love
Validate myself and choices

**CALM
PEACEFUL
CONTENT
FULFILLED
EASE
FOCUSED
OPTIMISTIC**

Presence to be here
Savour and appreciate this moment

As an adult you are responsible for fulfilling your own needs but if you don't recognise what you feel, it's hard to connect the dots with what you need. You can get stuck in everyone else's agenda for you or in pursuing things you think will satisfy you but don't because they're outside in instead of inside out.

Moving out of overwhelm and discovering balance is dynamic; it is always evolving. As your priorities shift and change and your life ebbs and flows you want to be able to feel the changing tides and decide what to prioritise to restore a sense of balance and flow for you.

When you feel that pull, it's an opportunity to stop and release the pressure. From this place you can notice the pulls and discern what's important.

Case Study

Focus on the here and now

Julia, 40s, married
Full-time, Head of HR.
Self-imposed limitation: "Push through and keep going"
Courage practice needed: Slow Down, Pause and Breathe

The core issue

"I don't know what to do. I just feel overwhelmed, I can't focus on anything. I am constantly rushing and not where I want to be in my career or life ..."

Julia came to coaching because she was stuck, overwhelmed, and wanted to feel better. She described physical symptoms of chronic tension: headaches, back and neck ache and tight jaw.

Relationships were strained. At home, she was in a debilitating cycle of bickering with her partner over seemingly insignificant things like the chores. They lost time and care arguing over the inequity of roles, competing over whose job was more demanding. Julia felt increasingly resentful about all the unappreciated things she did on top of her day job to make their home function.

At work she felt pulled in different directions, caught between stakeholders, debating the numbers, and playing a political, unfulfilling role. She wanted to focus on bringing more humanity to work but the organisation prioritised task, outcomes and profit over people and relationships. This deeply frustrated her, and she felt unable to fully utilise her skills or contribute effectively.

Julia felt the pressure of everything building up, needing to figure out what to do and where to focus next. She was stuck, overwhelmed, unable to think clearly or access her own insight and wisdom.

She dealt with this by dismissal and suppression, trying to put her best foot forward. But she had a constant internal conflict. Her strategy of bottling things up and acting as if it was all fine clashed with this feeling that it could be different. But her body experienced that suppression as pressure and tightened, her breath was high in her chest and she frequently held it, her jaw locked, and her shoulders and neck tensed up.

We began with the anchoring phase of the process and explored ways to help her get present, allow the pressure to be there and give it some space. She tried various breath and grounding practices. Julia noticed that she had been holding her breath all the time, even when she put the washing out!

As she practised regularly changing her breathing habits, she started to experience feelings of calm. She identified that she felt safest with people that acknowledged her feelings and validated her needs. She felt that didn't happen currently in her marriage or in her work.

The key was for her to learn to create that feeling of safety inside herself, so that she could tune in and discern how to fulfil her own needs. From this place she could then access the insight and wisdom from her emotional experience.

What Julia learnt

As she shifted her emotional experience, she was able to gain more clarity and insight. Ultimately, she identified the co-dependency in her relationship and discussed with her partner the opportunity for couples therapy.

Addressing the reality of her situation helped her to release the reaction to how things were at work and gradually begin to dream of a new possibility. She saw the toxicity of the culture she was working in and recognised that she didn't have the mandate to make significant change. Her efforts to harmonise and maintain good relationships were futile. This empowered Julia to dream about the type of organisation she would thrive in and then take proactive steps to manifest this change.

Julia recognised the need to establish a practice of grounding herself in her senses when she felt the overwhelm creeping up. This helped her to navigate and ride her emotional waves and navigate her own fearful thinking that previously kept her in the overwhelm.

She accepted the culture she was operating in and realised that she wanted to work in a different culture that supported diversity, psychological safety and relationships alongside profitability. This resulted in Julia getting a new job in a start-up that was beginning to scale up. She was able to shape the culture to support the founders' ambitions and whilst she didn't increase her financial package significantly, her fulfilment radically increased.

Slow Down, Pause and Breathe

Human beings are reactive much of the time. It is in the slowing down and getting present that you can see clearly. In a 24/7, permanently-on world it's easy to lose your own grounding and pace. When you're passionate, care deeply and are purpose driven, you can overextend yourself and get lost in the external needs that you see.

You may currently identify yourself as a multi-tasker or plate spinner. You may even have some of your self-worth tied up in your ability to achieve. To move from overwhelm will require a shift in this identity. Instead of being a woman who focuses on everything else and everyone else first, you can choose to put yourself first.

The challenge you may face is that you feel selfish and you claiming back space for yourself will impact those around you. Expect kickback. It is true that you can teach people how to treat you, and if up until now you haven't prioritised yourself or your need for space, quality time and focused action, people around you may be surprised at you changing the agenda.

To come out of overwhelm requires you to see the self-imposed limitation you have created for yourself and consciously change it. You need to know what your energy is and its limitations and discern what you want to give it to.

Slow down, pause and breathe

Create a habit of regularly slowing down, pausing, and consciously breathing.

Creating a habit like this will help you to tune in, anchor and connect to yourself. Without grounding you will be blown around by everyone else's agenda and needs, unable to access your own. It makes it hard to use your emotions as signals or packets of wisdom to guide you in discerning what you need. This in turn will make it challenging to speak your truth or hold clear boundaries.

Anchoring in your breath sets you up for success. It puts your body in the right frame to support you to do and be your best self. You can think clearly and focus on what is important.

An excellent way to develop consciously breathing is to use the Heartmath breathing technique. There is an audio session using this for you to follow, and it is on the Resources page on my website: https://courageunfolding. com/resources/

Ways to make this work:

Focus on the here and now

- The challenge is to create a new habit. You can do this by stacking a habit onto another one. For example, each time you have a drink, breathe.
- Another option is to set a regular reminder on your phone that simply says 'Breathe'.
- Notice where you're feeling overwhelmed or losing energy and decide to drop an anchor into you and get present within your body. From this place you can explore what you authentically need and in turn what to prioritise.

Draw on your inner strengths

CONNECT TO YOUR INNATE WORTHINESS

*When life is stuffed with unrealistically high expectations and constant doing you can lose sight of your strengths and resourcefulness in the drive to meet them. I share with you a **Build Core Strength** courage practice to reconnect to your knowledge, skills, experience and self-belief to guide you in the moment.*

———————

Living an authentically powered life is hard when you've built your self-worth around achievement, external success and validation. You feel that achievement and external praise are what's needed for you to feel good about yourself. Soul stamina is needed to make the shift to living authentically otherwise you will be at the constant mercy of seeking others' approval and validation.

You were born worthy

You bring value by being yourself. Your job is not to seek to attain perfection, because you already are perfectly imperfect. You were not born to shapeshift, adapt or fit in to the extent that you forget yourself.

When you have self-worth, you value your humanity and give yourself permission to shine as you are. Your thoughts, feelings and behaviours are all tied into your view of your worthiness and value as a human being. But the connection between your conditioning, self-worth and achievement can make worthiness feel like it comes from external sources. Your self-worth determines your life.

Self-worth theory suggests that your goal in life should be self-acceptance and that this is often found through achievement. You evaluate your self-worth based on your own self-appraisals. You will use different criteria, but common external ones include what you do, who you know, your appearance, what you achieve and your net worth.

In my survey, 54% of women stated that they frequently compared themselves less favourably to others. The problem with comparison is that it undermines self-worth because you aren't comparing like with like. You compare an idealised image which then provides a distorted perception. It takes you away from embracing your own unique essence.

Imposter syndrome

Perfected ideals, comparison, perfectionism and self-criticism are factors that women bring to coaching which are feeding this notion of being an imposter. It's common for them to compare themselves with other women and believe the image another woman is presenting without knowing or questioning the reality. They fantasise those other women are great at balancing everything, that they don't have struggles and that their images of perfection are real.

This then undermines their own evaluation of themselves. They are hard on themselves and even after they may have achieved the promotion they wanted, self-sabotage sets in by questioning, criticising and worrying that they will get found out as not being deserving of the position.

Self-awareness is key and the first step is to create awareness about how you naturally and authentically shine. You have needs, values, strengths and fears. Whenever you are at the edge of your comfort zone, fear and doubt will accompany you. It becomes a conscious choice – to value or to undermine yourself.

Imagine your fears, limiting belief, fantasies and comparisons are liabilities on a financial statement.

My personal balance sheet

ASSETS +	LIABILITIES –
Strengths – who I am	Fears – who I should be
Knowledge & skills	Limiting beliefs
Experience	Idealised images
Essence / Nature	Comparisons

If you focus on your liabilities rather than your assets, this causes you to push harder than you need, to prove yourself and to protect and defend your perceived vulnerabilities. If we focus on who we are not, or who we believe we should be, we end up trying to be something other than our authentic selves. A fear develops which drives us to mask our true self.

To anchor in yourself requires you to hold a mirror up and challenge if your focus is growing you or protecting you. Are you reacting to a limiting belief or fear? Are you projecting that limiting belief onto others, assuming that they will think you're not smart enough or some other version of not being enough?

A far more positive approach is to focus on your assets, your strengths, your values, and the other points in the balance sheet listed above. By being guided by these instead of our liabilities we own our authentic selves and what makes us unique without the hustle.

So, why not now create your own personal balance sheet, listing up to five in each area. Cherish and be proud of what you have placed in the assets area and reflect on what you have identified as liabilities. Are they true liabilities or simply limiting beliefs?

Assets

_____

_____

_____

Liabilities

_____

_____

_____

Your value lies within you

Imagine you are in a job of heading up a team. You're being counted on to deliver great ideas and campaigns that move the business forward. But there's an issue. Your team are frustrated and feeling like you are all over them. They feel they can't breathe around you.

Where does your value lie? You aren't going to improve your sense of worthiness by hustling. You can't please your team; they're unhappy and complaining. So, what do you do? What can you rely on?

The one thing you can rely on is yourself. You don't need to prove yourself. You simply need to embrace your full authentic self, knowing that you, like everyone else, are perfectly imperfect. In moments like this you need to dig deep and remind yourself of your strengths. The things you know yourself for. Everyone has a different combination of strengths, but the challenge is embracing them, owning them, and leading from them.

You improve your worthiness by realising what you have in yourself already, by becoming more of yourself. Maybe it's your empathy, perhaps it's your kindness, playfulness, eccentricity, warmth or your creativity. These are things that cannot be taken from or given to you. They're part of you.

There can be a tendency when you're in relationship with others who have different gifts and ways of being to want them to change to accommodate you. You focus your energy on giving them feedback and trying to suggest alternative ways they could say and do things. But this is giving your power away and it's reactive. The opportunity in these situations is for you to self-empower and advocate not by forcing your way but by being clear on what you feel and asking for what you need. This is how you let your team breathe! In doing so you also create psychological safety – your team now understands that they don't have to be perfect. It's now ok to fail and learn.

The journey you are on in this book is to rediscover who you are through the lens of positive appreciation. Why? So that you can let go of unhealthy ways of striving and reaction, accept your greatness and be more of yourself.

Whatever age you are now, can you own that you are perfectly perfect just as you are? Can you claim that you are brilliant, whole, and wildly successful in your own right?

Play to your strengths

A strength is something you love doing, you're good at and it gives you energy. You may have already discovered your strengths but often they get confused with what you have merely learnt to do well.

Identifying and owning your strengths is a wonderful discovery because it explains what helps you come alive and it's in using those strengths that you can get yourself into the flow state.

Through the education system, you may have focused on improving your weaknesses rather than playing to your strengths. You may also have found that your strengths were not realised because in education the emphasis is on academic attainment not on strengths spotting. It's outcome driven rather than focusing on the how and your being. When you focus on weaknesses your attention is on what's missing rather than what you already have.

You may have been brought up to be humble and feel awkward, shy or embarrassed about owning your strengths; after all, no one likes a big head or someone that's too much. Internalised, this feedback can create fear that you shouldn't be who you are and can cause you to repress your natural strengths.

The bottom line is that when you use your strengths, you feel happier, are more confident, have higher esteem and more energy, and build resilience.

How strengths relate to healthy/unhealthy striving

When you are in healthy striving you are honouring your strengths. You are focused on the areas that give you energy and as a result you feel good when you're using them. You're no longer trying to be something you're not and you feel a sense of congruence and authenticity because you're embracing what makes you unique.

When you are in unhealthy striving you are focusing on trying to prove yourself and get things right. Fear of not being enough and lack of self-acceptance create a relentless drive to achieve, which can ultimately lead to burnout. There's a pushing (or even punishing) energy to work and life and it's often accompanied by self-criticism and judgment.

You are working and living in an era where you are free to play to your strengths, but sometimes old myths still operate. You do not need to be a good all-rounder. You need to be more of yourself because that is where you stand out and shine. It's where you'll have your biggest impact and make the difference you crave.

And the good news is, the more you appreciate your strengths the more it has a multiplier effect. If I may use my own experience as an example to illustrate here – I am a big picture person, intuitive and creative and I am not particularly structured or detailed. Many of the organisations I have worked in turned out to be stodgy bureaucracies that espoused a desire for innovation and vision but stuck to convention and rigid procedures.

I once worked for a boss who was highly structured and detailed. She wanted all the t's crossed and i's dotted. It was a nightmare for me, and I would spend hours getting increasingly anxious proofreading and looking for errors. Liberation only happened when I accepted that I could just focus on playing to my strength of strategic thinking. I realised that it was ok not to be detailed and that within the organisation there were people who had detail as a strength who could be delegated to undertake the analytical work.

I knew that I had finally let go of trying to be someone I wasn't when a co-lead said to a room of 60 senior managers that I was rubbish with detail. I laughed and agreed, knowing that I had healed this part of me that had me believe I had to hide my weaknesses. I no longer felt the 'ouch' moment of perceiving it as a weakness; instead, I owned my strength and explained to the room that this was what helped me embrace my leadership.

Identify your strengths

The first step involves opening to discovering your strengths. There are many strengths profiles available, and all have their merits. I personally use Strengths Profile (strengthsprofile.com) because it provides a useful framework and language that helps you discover and be your best self every day.

The profile is divided into four areas of focus: realised strengths, unrealised strengths, learned behaviours, and weaknesses. These give you a way of seeing yourself as an energy system and help you understand why your energy gets depleted doing certain tasks and renewed doing others.

Once you're clear about your strengths you can practise and harness them so that you manage your energy in a whole different way. Instead of focusing on improving your weaknesses it is recommended that you find strategies for them. Learned behaviours are things you are good at but don't energise you, so the recommendation is that you use them consciously and not all the time.

If this is not something you wish to pursue, another option is to ask people close to you at work and at home what your impact is or what they appreciate and rely on in you. This is a lovely exercise to do anyway as it gives you information that isn't readily shared unless their 'love language' happens to be words of affirmation. As an aside, the nature of your love language is well worth exploring, and I have found The 5 Love Languages a great place to start, at 5lovelanguages.com. However, if you only take this approach the results are limited to their observation and awareness.

The beauty of undertaking a strength profile is that, as well as gaining the opinion of others, you can reveal your personal impact and discover a whole new way of understanding and managing your energy system.

Strengths give you choice and empowerment. You can choose consciously to focus on what gives you energy, what you're great at and what you enjoy, which in turn helps you to feel good and be at your best.

They enable you to have a different mindset where work is not just a passive task that you have to complete to get paid. You cultivate a mindset where you know yourself from the inside out, what brings you alive and what makes you strong and how you can achieve your best performance at work and at home. This in turn gives you the opportunity to be more discerning with what you say yes and no to, and the responsibility to choose situations and environments that support you playing to your strengths.

Understanding your strengths opens your choices. It helps you to advocate for yourself in a completely different way because you know where your brilliance lies.

Case Study

Draw on your inner strengths

Dawn, late 30s, single
Full-time, Marketing Manager
Self-imposed limitation: "I'm afraid I'm not smart enough"
Courage practice needed: Build Core Strength

The core issue:

"I try so hard to help people in the team, but they don't appreciate it. I'm starting to feel resentful and overwhelmed. I can't figure out, am I the problem, or are they?"

Dawn was a fabulous spark of energy that always greeted you with a smile and radiated positivity. Her attitude was that there was always a solution and that sometimes you just had to look hard to find it. Recently she had started to question her impact.

Her team were struggling to keep up with her and Dawn would leap into doing the job herself because often it was just quicker and easier. Besides, she had done every job in the department, so she knew what to do. But the unintended impact was her team felt undermined and, feeling unable to talk to Dawn about it, they had started to complain to people outside the team.

This gossiping triggered insecurity in Dawn. She came to me questioning if she was the problem or if her team were the problem. She felt hurt, resentful and angry. Dawn's limiting belief that had unconsciously been triggered was that she was not smart enough. Thinking that belief made her feel self-conscious and ashamed, so she began to withdraw further.

Dawn had lost sight of her strengths and her value to the team. She was caught in a spiral of negative thinking and reactive feeling. To help her move out of this cycle she first had to accept what was going on and explore where she had influence.

As we examined the roots of her limiting belief, she saw it was a story she had created in childhood. During her formative years she was set incredibly high standards by her mother, who rewarded her for achievement and criticised her for her failures. Her mother had set a high bar for herself, and her success compounded Dawn's acceptance of the need to strive to be the best.

Being faced with a reality that her own behaviours were having an unintended leadership impact was incredibly confronting for her. A part of her wanted to blame the team. Another part of her wanted to blame herself for her failure as a leader. She came to work with me because she felt her efforts were failing her and she wanted to figure out whose issue it was.

Part of our work together involved retiring the blame story and helping her create a new story that was built on a platform of self-acceptance. When she explored her strengths, she realised that many of them were in the strategic elements of the work. She was great at inspiring and painting a vision and seeing the interconnection of things.

In accepting her strengths she started to accept her unique value in setting direction and stakeholder management within the team. She defined the gap in the skillset of the team where the delivery needed a different type of overseeing. The decision to recruit a new team member with organisation, planning and detail strengths complemented the team and filled a gap in the pipeline.

What Dawn learnt

Firstly, to question the measurements she was using to evaluate herself against and check that it wasn't coming from her inner critic's or someone else's standard. Being aware of her old narrative of fear of not being smart enough helped her turn towards the frightened little girl inside her who carried this story and felt inadequate, and soothe her. She reminded the little girl that she was an adult who had gained much knowledge about her strengths and brilliance and that everything was exactly as it was supposed to be.

She created a new story about her strengths, brilliance, and vision of who she was becoming. This resulted in her taking things less personally when her team acted up or she received feedback. It empowered her to believe in her humanity, perfect imperfection, strength and natural brilliance.

Courage Practice:

Build Core Strength

You can choose what you focus on and bring your strengths to it. Make leaning into your strengths a new habit. To enable that you need to consciously practise building your mental strength. If you were doing some physical training, you would complete tests to gauge your strength, flexibility and conditioning. So, in the same way, you need to keep evaluating your mental core strength.

In work and life, you have the potential to draw on many strengths. Working explicitly with one strength will help you deepen your awareness, understand how to best utilise it and identify the conditions necessary for you to consciously draw on it. For example, a strength of creativity might need a relaxed environment of play.

Build your core strength

- Pick one strength that you are consciously going to embrace and utilise during this week.
- Every time you do something, use that strength to support you.
- At the end of the day write down 3 bullet points of how you've used that strength and the impact of that. There is a table for you to enter your own initial version of this, plus overleaf is an example of how I used one of my strengths, creativity and summarised its use:

Strength	Environment	Impact
Creativity – I consciously chose to use this in a team meeting where we were stuck in traditional thinking	I used colour, Lego bricks and Post-it notes to explore options	I felt lightness and ease when I used this strength It brought new ideas to the team that they could build upon It felt less like a chore and more enjoyable

Strength

_____

_____

_____

_____

_____

Environment

_____

_____

_____

_____

_____

Impact

_____

_____

_____

_____

_____

_____

Ways to make this work:

Draw on your inner strength

- Your worth comes from understanding, loving, and accepting yourself as you are.
- Change happens as you embrace and become more of who you are.
- Practise worthiness from within by noticing when you're pushing and pivoting to trust in your innate strengths and essence.

Audit

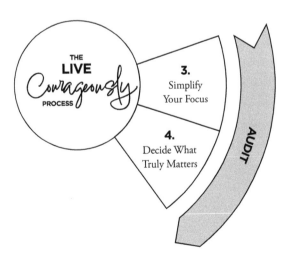

Simplify your focus

INCREASE AWARENESS OF WHAT DRIVES YOU

When your head is full you can't focus clearly. Completing a **Be Intentional** *courage audit will help you discern what's driving you and what to prioritise to create meaningful change. Choosing consciously where to put the focus of your attention is the focus of this courage practice.*

Stressors will always be present in your life; know what drives them and how you can choose to respond to them.

Your response-ability

As I've mentioned, humans often resist being in the overwhelm, with all its difficulty, fear, and frustration. Why sit feeling overwhelmed when you could turn your attention towards fixing it? But if your reaction to every situation that is uncomfortable or frustrating is that it must be fixed, you are losing so much valuable time and effort.

It's easy to think that the problem is the situation and to put all your effort into changing or fixing it. But that desire to always try to fix it is a reaction to something that's difficult and it's only when you explore your own hard places that you will find your best learning and transformation.

Instead, think about adopting 100% response-ability, which means being where you are now and being able to choose consciously how you respond instead of letting emotional storms create chaos.

When you feel emotionally overwhelmed, your stress hormones hijack your internal system, making it impossible to think straight or make good decisions. It's a human reaction to keep doing what you've always done and strive to take on more, but this doesn't work.

How work and life become cluttered

Imagine that when you come into this world you have a clean slate and an empty wardrobe. Over time and as you grow, people (parents, teachers, authority figures) give you items to put into your wardrobe. These items include beliefs, rules, habits and ways of being. How you should be in the world to stay safe and attain happiness.

Your safety and belonging are the primary function of these items. If you follow the rules and expectations that have been set for you, you will be safe and accepted within your family unit and wider culture. These beliefs, rules and habitual ways of being will have served you in getting you where you are today so, until a crisis point, they remain in the wardrobe, largely unquestioned.

Also included in the wardrobe are your emotional habits. These are rules and beliefs which have formed the structure within your wardrobe. The primary role of your inner critic is to keep you safe by enforcing that structure and its rule book.

Audit and declutter

Auditing and decluttering life is not a regular practice for human beings. In the Western world our capitalist culture has us seek quick fixes and solutions instead of encouraging us to slow down our thinking and examine our biases, assumptions and responsibilities.

It takes a great deal of courage to be open to the idea that the way your life is structured might not be supporting who you are, how you want to be or what you want to do. If you can let someone into what's really running you under the surface, you have the opportunity to reveal some wisdom.

You need to embrace the bits you want to cover up because it's those bits that make us deeply human. Think of it this way: you are an infinite being weaving patterns of life. Many of these patterns you're weaving will be unconscious to you.

Perhaps you've created a pattern of unconscious busyness. When things get tricky or there are too many demands on you, instead of slowing down to reflect and take stock, you dig in and keep soldiering on. You do what you've always done because that is the way it's supposed to be done! It's the way you've observed in those around you, or perhaps you unconsciously decided it for yourself. That is until what you've done no longer works for you.

When a catalyst happens in your life, it provides the moment to re-evaluate but to do this you need to stop running at 90mph. The challenge is that your fear causes you to cling to what is known and stay firmly in your comfort zone. But if you see the catalyst as an opportunity to review, you can become an observer and evaluate if the way you're working is supporting you in the direction you want to go.

Begin by slowing down

In my survey, time and creating discrete space away from the day-to-day grind were two of the most frequently identified factors preventing women from valuing and putting themselves first. 53% of women reported that there is never enough time and that they prioritise others' needs ahead of their own.

The obvious way to do this is to stop trying to be permanently 'on' at work and at home and start getting good rest and renewal. I cannot tell you how many clients come to coaching in a state of overwhelm and exhaustion and resist this slowing down and replenishment. They will say things like, "How am I meant to do that when there's so much to do?" or "I'll slow down when I've got this done" or "I need to speed up, not slow down" or "I work for an American sales company, and they demand that you are always on."

You lose something when you fill everything up. If you cram everything into your life, there is no space to move. My intention here isn't to convince you to change. The important thing is that if something in your life isn't working for you, the place to begin is to slow down so that you can press pause and take stock.

When you step outside yourself you can discern and see clearly but when you're hurtling through life with unexamined beliefs, assumptions, rules, and expectations of how it should be, it's damned hard to get off that track.

There is a beauty in laying out your life in front of you and examining the different aspects. You get to take each item in your wardrobe and hold it up and ask if it is serving you to hold on to it. You can question the purpose and value it has within your life and decide whether you keep it as it is, change an aspect or completely let it go.

In holding each aspect up to consider it more deeply, you not only acknowledge its presence in your life, but you also notice the impact it has. So, whether that's a belief like "I have to be nice", an expectation like "I must be perfect" or an emotional habit like "I can't express anger" you get to decide if that's true for you.

Unless you slow down, you won't see these silent rules and operating systems that drive your behaviours. It's about creating space in your wardrobe because if you're always putting more in, you can never decide if what's in there is what you want.

Creating space by slowing down is a vulnerable act because it involves embracing the parts that you want to cover up. Simply admitting that you're emotionally overwhelmed gives you an opportunity to handle that differently because you've opened a new possibility. You can then decide whether you want to continue in that place or try something new.

The conditioned vs the soul path

I believe there are two paths: the conditioned path and the soul path. On the conditioned path there can be a narrative that says I have to behave in a certain way towards power or authority, elders, other people etc. You have rules in your head that have you suck things up rather than empower you.

If we take the example of working for an American company on a different time zone, I have seen European teams burnt out by the idea that they must react to their leaders' demands. It has meant they work crazy hours and are always on. They default to overwhelm and complaint and decide this is just the way it must be.

But in truth, there is a conversation needed to acknowledge the different time zones and decide how to set up working practices to respect each other's rest and renewal so that they can do even better work together. Furthermore, there's a recognition that when one person who is at the start of their day talks to another person at the end of their day, there will be a difference in energy and capacity to respond. If we acknowledge the reality and embrace the differences, we can then design how we want to be together around it.

The same process is true for your soul path. If you slow down, rest and renew you can begin to listen deeply within yourself. You can hear what wants to unfold and you find out what lights you up and feels aligned and resonant to your authenticity.

Your soul is always calling you to remember who you are and your true path

You know when things feel off. But you've probably trained yourself out of trusting yourself. When you want to fit in and belong you can forget who you are and what you stand for.

Being busy, distracted, overwhelmed or underwhelmed are all convenient strategies to stay stuck in a repetitive and reactive cycle. Slow down to see the system you are in and give yourself a new kind of freedom. You may decide to stay in the same pattern, or you may choose a different set of priorities. Either way you will come from conscious awareness and that will serve you in living your life, your way.

It's surprising how many clients defend their current reality without fully exploring it. Instead of putting their creative energy into forward momentum they get caught in unconscious defensiveness, reacting to how it is and arguing how it shouldn't be that way but that's the only way it can be. The unacknowledged emotions and beliefs that underpin everything keep them stuck.

Don't believe me? Think about it for a moment. How many times have you been unhappy with a situation but when someone asks you what you want you revert to telling them how it is and all the reasons why it is the way it is?

Often my clients say to me they want a quick fix. I've even had clients say how they wished there was a pill that would just take away all the pain and make them stop thinking negatively. But the thing about pain is that whilst we might numb it, it has a funny habit of coming back up to the surface.

It's in this place that you can get tunnel thinking, where you're stuck in a cycle of self-limiting thinking that the more you keep thinking about it the further down the tunnel you go. You may be lost in busyness and stuck in mental ruminations. Or perhaps you're overwhelmed by feelings arising from the experience you're in.

To create movement requires an honest appraisal of what's occurring and what's beneath that.

Now take a Be Intentional courage audit

Regularly auditing your beliefs, emotions and actions will help you to clarify what's creating the results you have. Courage in work and life involves regular review, active prioritisation, and action towards your goals.

Clarity gives perspective about what you want and what's preventing movement towards your goal. To gain clarity you need to identify what limits your courage and how this determines your behaviours.

Begin by considering the courage audit questions opposite, which cover the areas of beliefs, behaviours and habits in each of the areas in the wheel later in this chapter.

Please note that there is a second copy of this courage audit form at the end of this book, giving you the option to complete a second version of this in, say, one year's time, to track changes in your responses as you work through the Live Courageously Process.

	Always	Sometimes	Never
Opinion beliefs:			
My opinion matters			
My knowledge, skills and experience have value			
My feelings count			
My needs and requests are important			
Opinion behaviours:			
I communicate what I see, sense and feel			
I raise concerns			
I ask for what I need			
I make clear requests			
Authority beliefs:			
I am my own best authority			
I trust my intuition			
I am equal in my work relationships regardless of status and power			
I make my own choices			

	Always	Sometimes	Never
Authority behaviours:			
I empower myself and make decisions			
I navigate through fear and doubt			
I stand my ground with strong personalities			
I have self-respect and authenticity			
Personal growth beliefs:			
I am always learning and growing			
There is no failure, only failing to try			
Growth is possible in everything			
The only person I can change is myself			
Personal growth behaviours:			
I set myself goals for what I want to achieve			
I focus on growing my skills and competencies			
I recognise and walk through my learning edges			
I challenge and support myself in equal measures			

	Always	Sometimes	Never
Emotional mastery beliefs:			
All of my emotions are valid			
My emotions deliver information to me			
My emotions are neither good nor bad			
I can master my emotions			
Emotional mastery behaviours:			
I name my emotions			
I process my emotions without defaulting to analysis			
I explore the wisdom my emotions give me			
I can change my emotional state			
Worthiness beliefs:			
I define what success means to me			
I am enough as I am			
I have unique strengths			
I am innately worthy			
I believe in myself			

	Always	Sometimes	Never
I am worthy of career advancement			
Worthiness behaviours:			
I prioritise what matters to me in my career and life			
I advocate for myself			
I pursue career advancement			
Fun and recreation beliefs:			
I am the creator of my own experience			
Fun and joy matter to my life			
I can achieve the right balance for me between work and fun			
I can prioritise enjoyment			
Fun and recreation behaviours:			
I prioritise and schedule fun			
I choose activities that light me up			
I am present and in the moment during recreation activities			
I surround myself with people that lift me			

	Always	Sometimes	Never
Boundary beliefs:			
I am allowed to set my own boundaries and tell people what's ok and what isn't			
It's ok to stand up for my preferences and work-life balance			
I choose who to be in relationship with			
I do not have to carry other people's emotional baggage			
Boundary behaviours:			
I set clear boundaries			
I confront bad behaviour			
I do not tolerate poor excuses or people that invalidate my feelings			
I give what's required (not over-giving)			
Accountability beliefs:			
I create my own outcomes			
I create my own psychological safety			
Trust is an inside job			
I am responsible for my own actions			
If I'm accountable, I'm more likely to do what I say I will do			

	Always	Sometimes	Never
I can only be responsible for what I can influence			
Accountability behaviours:			
I keep my word to myself			
I don't overpromise			
I act decisively			
I do what I say I will do			
I declare my accountability, to myself and to others			
I hold others accountable, where appropriate			
I avoid apportioning blame			
I focus on being responsible for things I can influence and change			

Audit reflection

Having completed the Be Intentional courage audit, ask yourself what are the beliefs, rules and laws that you make for yourself that stop you from fully stepping into your courage?

Having completed the reflection, select your overall satisfaction level for each area of your life in the balance wheel of life opposite, with 1 being that you are unsatisfied and 10 being that you are happy in this area.

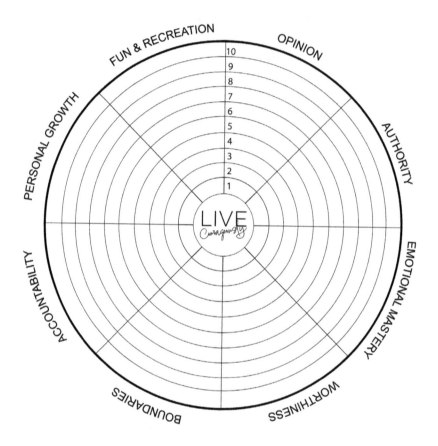

You are now in a clear position to discern where you want to prioritise your efforts.

Case Study

Simplify your focus

Kate, late 40s, married
Full-time, Project Manager
Self-imposed limitation: "I must not be angry"
Courage practice needed: Be Intentional

The core issue

"My life is like a wardrobe. It's stuffed with so many things at work and home that I can't shut the door on it. Just opening the door makes me feel depressed and hopeless. And I'm not even sure I like the things in it anymore..."

Kate was a project manager in a technical company. Her role relied on her communication and relationship skills, as she walked a fine line between multiple stakeholders to get things done. She often found her days long and emotionally draining, particularly when it felt like she was dealing with constant rebuttals from technical architects and engineers who saw the world very differently to salespeople and customers.

Life at home was tough, with two teenagers who were often unreasonable in their expectations. Her husband often said that it was like walking on eggshells between hers and their teenagers' moods.

Kate found herself frequently losing her temper and screaming at her kids, only to later sit in her bedroom and feel guilt and remorse. This added to her stress levels. Being perimenopausal, she also knew her hormones were wreaking havoc on her but knowing that didn't help because she felt like there was little she could do about it. At work, she could see the validity in everyone's perspective, but she couldn't find a resolution. She felt like she was often in a mental fog.

It didn't help that she worked for a young, dynamic tech company. This added to the pressure. She was the oldest in her team and she felt embarrassed about not being able to get a handle on things. She certainly didn't feel able to talk about any of this with her boss.

Kate had figured out that the best thing she could do was to keep on going. But recently she'd become stuck and was struggling to manage her emotions. Her inner self-talk had become increasingly critical. She'd always been tough on herself but now it felt like she was shaming herself by telling herself what a screw-up she was when things didn't go well.

Under normal circumstances, Kate probably wouldn't have reached out for coaching. She liked to be seen as capable and in control and vulnerability wasn't her modus operandi. She preferred stoicism and independence as her approach.

But when her manager pulled her aside and gave her some candid feedback about changes he'd seen in her and the impact on her work, she knew she needed to talk things through and refocus. Her hurt pride made her want to quit but she needed this job and she'd worked hard to get where she was.

In our first conversation Kate cried, as she dumped everything on the table: how she felt, the fears she had, the confusion and lack of clarity and her deep-seated fear that she would get fired and her husband would leave because he'd had enough.

Kate had plenty of reasons why she was where she was and in that situation. As she offloaded, she also found herself justifying why she thought it had to be this way. It was clear that Kate was embedded in her current situation to the extent that she couldn't see any wider perspective. She couldn't tell me how she wanted to feel because she was locked in her fears.

Kate's unconscious rule was "Must not be angry". When her stresses accumulated to the point that she couldn't contain them, she would explode and then her critic would judge her according to the rule of "must not be angry" and give her a hard time. It wasn't until things started to fall apart that she was willing to look at and question what was going on. This opened a doorway into examining her inner psychology and through that she was able to take charge consciously.

For Kate the feedback and subsequent threat of potentially losing her job further down the line if she didn't step up was her catalyst moment. She knew she had to put a line in the sand and do things differently. To get perspective Kate had to audit where she was. She started by using a simple balance wheel, similar to one I have illustrated earlier.

When Kate mapped out the bigger picture of her life, she identified that the key area for her to work on was personal growth. She saw that what was running her at work was also running her at home and it came from a behaviour that she identified as her "passive appeasement".

Rather than thinking logically, being clear on her intentions and taking decisions from this place, she was defaulting to appeasement. She was listening too much to the many divergent perspectives and she had lost faith in her own expert opinion. She wasn't standing in her power; she was unconsciously giving her power to others. She was then feeling overwhelmed by her frustration.

Kate's challenge was her unconscious need to seek permission and approval. She wanted to be liked and to please others and was concerned by what others thought. Acceptance and belonging mattered to her and she wanted to make a good impression. That meant she would say and do things to win approval and hide her real feelings at the cost of her own agenda for her life.

But the thing with approval-seeking is that no one in history has ever been universally approved of. It's an unrealistic expectation of yourself that everyone will approve, endorse, or even support who you are and the choices you make in this world. I will explore this further in the chapter but for now I invite you to consider that anyone who's done anything amazing has been attacked and criticised at some point for it.

Kate's priorities became increasing her self-awareness and self-regard so that she could discover her own truth, opinion, and authenticity. She began the work of liking herself for who she already was and acknowledging her unique essence and strengths. Part of this meant finding creative ways to manage her anxiety and the inner critic that this feeling invoked. It also involved learning practical skills of assertiveness and conflict resolution.

Kate also needed to take charge of the stage of life she was in. Perimenopause is a time where your hormones create many changes in mood, confidence and overall well-being. Recognising that and seeking appropriate medical advice supported her to make small changes to her diet, explore hormone replacement treatment options, increase her exercise and have better boundaries with her time and energy.

What Kate learnt

Firstly, to slow down and audit her internal operating system against the results she had and the results she wanted. She started to ask herself the questions, "Whose rules am I observing? Are these supporting what I want to feel?" She began to process her emotion by moving her body through it. She would either exercise, run or do a yoga pose like the child's pose to support her to feel the feeling.

When she had moved through the feeling, she would explore her unmet need, expectation, or request behind it. This in turn helped her to take charge, set herself reasonable goals that embraced her energetic reality, and stop sweating the small stuff. She was able to talk with her manager about her challenges from a place of advocating for her needs, which resulted in increased understanding and clarity about modifications to make in her workplace to support her through the perimenopause into menopause.

Be Intentional

As I have said, stressors accumulate. Individual requests for your time and attention may seem innocuous but unless there is a habit of prioritising and de-prioritising, you can find yourself adapting to everyone else's agendas.

Being conscious and intentional about what you are focused on matters. You must choose your own lane. Anyone can get stuck in what's happened and what's next. True freedom is the freedom to choose, and it is a function of awareness.

Clarify your expectations of yourself each day; check in at regular intervals and ask:

- What's my motive?
- What's my intention?

Ways to make this work

Simplify your focus

- You always have a choice but sometimes you need to remind yourself of your own choice and agency.
- Design your life and the focus of your attention and energy.
- Set your own outcomes, expectations, and limits.
- If you notice you're feeling resentful or frustrated, pause, go back to the previous step and drop your anchor. Then check in with yourself and enquire within yourself as to what's running you.

Decide what truly matters

EMPOWER YOURSELF TO LIVE ACCORDING TO YOUR TRUTH

*Our world is noisy, with constant subliminal messaging that pushes our behaviour towards consumerism and markets to our insecurities. The courage practice **Live Your Values** will support you to reclarify and prioritise what matters to you.*

———————

Tuning out of the external noise and connecting with yourself takes space, grounding, compassion, courage and conscious choice.

Values are what truly matter to you

Values enable you to meet your own emotional needs (to belong, feel safe and secure and be fulfilled) by choosing to focus on the aspects that give you fulfilment. Values are what you place importance upon and how you prioritise that in your life.

Original values may have been handed down to you through your culture and conditioning. For example, humility may have been considered important in your family of origin. You accept this value as a norm because it's what you needed to do to fit into your tribe. Perhaps you were rewarded for being humble and letting others go first. These values can go unquestioned through life and simply become the way you do things.

Whilst the work of unearthing your values probably sounds simple, it's easy to let your conditioning get in the way. You choose what you think you ought to instead of what you want. To combat this resistance to explore requires a willingness to open to the not knowing and to the discovery of something new, giving yourself permission to be curious and truly honest. It can feel disloyal to let go of what you were told to value. It can feel like you're somehow going against the grain but it's in the questioning that you truly find what matters to you. This is a place where you can practise drawing on your courage – to have a beginner's mind, to not know and to discover anew.

Once you've decided on this path, you then have the responsibility to hold yourself accountable to let go of the values that do not fit you and honour the ones that do. Your values sit in your heart, not your head, so quietening the mind is necessary to identify them. Being present and grounded will help you to connect to your truth and trust your intuition.

When I asked questions in my survey about the ease of changing and sticking to new habits, a theme emerged that said it was dependent upon what the individual was trying to change and how important that was for them.

One of the bravest things you can do is question and consciously decide what matters to you. This simple exercise can take you to the edge of your comfort zone. Fear can have you cling to what is known and try to figure it all out. Doubt can have you question what's true for you. You may notice the urge to dismiss the exercise because it's vulnerable to admit that you don't know what truly makes you feel alive. A simple way to deal with this fear is to ask what type of fear it is. Is it illusory or is it a survival fear? The likelihood is that it's illusory and as such you can choose to pivot your attention into exploration and discovery.

Exploring fulfilment may feel scary because it forces you to identify the criteria that light you up, and once you've located them, you're faced with the decision to choose consciously. You may find that you're surrounded by mirrors reflecting your own life, people who reinforce your fears because they too are unconsciously choosing a path limited by their fears or unexamined rules and conditions. You decide, and in doing so, you become the adult and creator in your own life.

Discovering your values – my own case study

During the process of my separation and divorce I was faced with this huge uncertainty in my life. I had imagined life moving in a totally different direction to what was now unfolding. There was a dream that had suddenly disappeared which was accompanied by an awareness that no one could or should rescue me from this. I had to get myself through it.

Up until the breakup I had thought I was clear on my values. My work as a coach had afforded me plenty of opportunity to clarify and develop my sense of what mattered to me. But here I was, suddenly uprooting my life because I no longer felt that our marriage could work in the circumstances. To make that decision I leaned into my values of honesty and integrity and made them trump my need to feel safe and belong to something even if it was proven to be dysfunctional.

I knew that a few things mattered to me, nature and light being two of those. But letting go was much harder than I thought it would be. It wasn't the physical things that I had to let go of that were hard but the memories and experiences. It was as if the past had this romantic hold on me, despite this compelling need and urgency to move forward anew. In my dark moments I would harp back to how things had been and then catastrophise about the future – what if I was making the wrong decision, what if this was as good as it gets?

The first part of my new journey was to find a new house. I couldn't afford a house of my dreams, so I settled for a house that was near to where we used to live and my daughter's school, and agreed with myself that this was not my forever house but instead for a period of five years. When I moved in, I had this overwhelming fear that I'd made the wrong decision. I could hear the neighbours through the walls and the vulnerable part of me just wanted to retreat and live somewhere secluded. I had to soothe those fears and not dive into them.

I had no clue how I wanted to furnish it. It was a small house and I had very little that I had taken from our previous home. I explored colours, textures and designs but for a long time I had no real enthusiasm and no clue of what I liked.

I started taking photos of things I liked. Sometimes it would be that golden light on a tree just before sunset, or little ornaments, pictures, pieces of furniture. I began to create a montage of all the things that gave me joy. With each photo I pondered what it was about it that I loved. I started to see that light and a feeling of fresh airiness mattered to me.

My procrastination was irritating to my family. They wanted to see me settled and would push me to decide on furnishings. But what I learnt was that when I was pushed to decide I ended up returning the item because it didn't feel right.

I was discovering my likes and dislikes and as I sat in the enquiry of what I wanted, I noticed a pattern that I didn't like in myself. I would ask my girls or my mother what they thought and then if I went with their decision, I would be irritated with myself because I knew it wasn't quite right for me.

My illusory fear was that the girls wouldn't want to stay with me if the house wasn't right for them. It caused me to defer and try to please. This behaviour was deeply rooted in a fear of rejection and abandonment and a need for love and belonging.

As time moved on, I started to see something different in my procrastination and uncertainty. I noticed, if I stopped judging myself for my indecision, that there was a reason for it. I wasn't clear and until I was clear, I refused to act. This refusal stopped me from repeating old patterns of just reacting, and allowed me to develop a new inner confidence in my knowing. The more I waited patiently for something to unfold, the more an intuition and knowing would reveal itself to me.

Letting go of the need to know helped me unfold my truth. I was surprised to see that a new value was emerging in me. It was a value of beauty. I wanted to live in beauty. It wasn't a perfected beauty; it was a natural imperfect beauty.

As I began to unfold what this value of beauty meant to me, I saw key elements: clarity, light, symmetry, colour, vibrancy and heart were all aspects of this value but there was something deeper.

To appreciate beauty, I needed certain inner qualities. I needed to let go of judgement (of myself and others) to see the beauty in myself and in them. I had to turn towards gratitude to appreciate what was beautiful in the pain. I had to use an appreciative enquiry and unconditional positive regard to look for and find the beauty in myself and others.

What seemed on the surface a superficial value was revealing itself to me as a deeply profound way of being in the world. If I truly honoured beauty in my life, I had to release my self-judgement and harsh criticism that my search for beauty was a perfectionistic management of my anxiety and instead see that it was a way of walking through life in a calm, grounded and more patient way.

If I honoured beauty I had to trust in the natural unfolding and get beyond my Aries/Falcon (my birth totem) impatience to ignite everything now. It involved managing a tension that I felt through the seasons. For example, when you feel heavy from the dark nights of winter and long for spring, but you can't force it to come faster.

When I leaned into beauty as a value, I began to appreciate the need for rest and noticing the signs of spring on its way. I could hold that anxious, tense feeling of wanting to be through to the other side and into a new fresher energy.

Enquiring into the resonance of this energy I found a number of values encompassed within this overarching one of beauty. They encompassed the following areas:

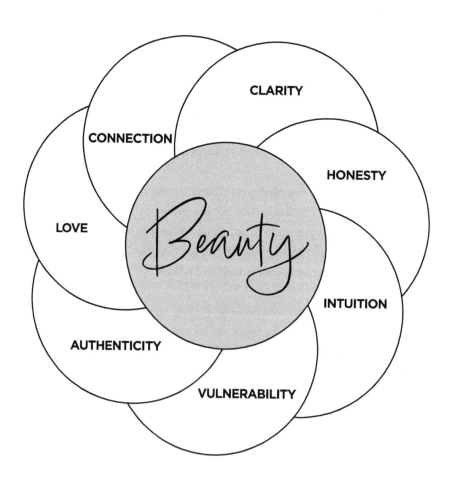

As I decided to consciously choose beauty more in my life, I saw a shift happening in my relationships. It became clearer for me to see what mattered, who I wanted to be in relationship with and who I didn't. In turn that made managing my boundaries easier. I had a clarity of what and who to say yes and no to in my life.

This newfound clarity gave a new depth to my consciousness and in turn gave me agency to walk and act in the world with intention. I didn't have to react to my pain and loss and could instead pivot and see the wisdom and insight my breakup had provided. I was deciding to live differently and the only way I could honour that decision was to change how I was with myself.

Up until that point I had lived my life with conditioning and learned behaviours of grit, drive, work ethic and harmonising. Those behaviours were fear based. The unconscious fear was revealed that if I stood up for the beauty I valued, I might be ridiculed or judged.

Having this new clarity, I was choosing and deciding to act with integrity and knowing towards what I knew mattered to me in life. I had a new compass to navigate from and the more I used it, the more my confidence in myself grew. It was a new kind of inside-out confidence which was based on an acceptance of who I was becoming and how I wanted to shape my life moving forward.

The walls of my house are now white which gives it a light, airy feel. It also means the paintings and colours that I have put into it stand out. It is not cluttered. The objects within it have meaning, like my shamanic drum and the representations of power animals which include a cockerel, goose and ram. These give me a feeling of inner peace, ease and safety. That feeling of safety was felt by my daughter's friend who said how she loved coming to my house and how she always felt safe in it.

The beauty value also connected to my work. I didn't want to do associate work that didn't align with my core values simply because it paid the bills. I was becoming passionate about working with women to support them to unfold their courage so that they could transform their relationships and their work. That knowing gave me the persistence I needed to overcome my doubts and write this book. Whilst this book involves my story and I found that it was healing parts of myself as I wrote it, it is also designed to provide a framework for other women to get into the right relationship with themselves and claim their authentic soulful paths. At many points in the writing process I judged myself as procrastinating and defaulting to others' opinions but beyond that judgment was a truth that I held on to that, if women hear other women's stories it creates connection and through that courage.

Define your values

Hopefully, through my lived example you can see there are some prerequisites that will support your discovery of your own values.

- **Be willing not to know.** Curiosity is fostered in a culture of non-judgement. Being willing to let something emerge is hard for humans who like certainty. Consciously choosing not knowing will allow knowing to unfold.
- **Give yourself permission to become an observer,** noticing that where you feel resonance, increased energy and aliveness requires observation and patience.
- **There is no right answer, only the one that comes from deep within you.** You've seen how I define beauty. You might have the same word for a completely different set of criteria. Trust yourself as you go through the journey of mining for your values. The exercise which follows explains how you can do that.

Values mining exercise

1. Think of a peak moment in your life when you felt a sense of flow; you were loving being in this experience. It's a moment that is etched in your memory and when you bring it to mind you will notice that

you were so caught in the moment that you lost a sense of time. You were fully present in this situation.

2. Brainstorm and write down what the values were that were in this situation. You may have a thought that the feeling was created because it was the situation. Look beyond this thought and the situation. What was it about that time that made it feel special to you or gave you a feeling of aliveness?

3. Now do the opposite. Think of a moment in your life when you felt stuck or lost in ever decreasing circles. What was missing in that moment? What wasn't being honoured? Write down the values that were missing that come up from this place.

4. Take the list of value words that you have written down and organise them into a string of what sits together. I gave you my example of beauty being the core value and its component parts of clarity, honesty, intuition etc. You are undertaking the same process and finding your own words and language for your values.

5. Sit with the values for 2 weeks. Track yourself to see whether your key moments during this time relate to your identified values.

6. Go back and refine your list. Identify your top 3 core values – the three things that you simply must have. Mine are clarity (and I include honesty in that), intuition and love. I trust that when I honour these I walk in my own authentic beauty.

7. Create a visual board of images that represents your top 3 values. This imagery will help you to symbolise and recall your values.

8. You will find that just holding 3 values is challenging. There will be times when your values clash with each other. You will also find that there will be times when your values clash with another person's. This gives you choice to lean into your curiosity and understand what's creating conflict and then actively prioritise and choose what you honour or let go of. Your values don't tend to change over time but the priority you give them will vary. Prioritising which values you are choosing to honour in particular situations will help you to practise walking through your day with your value in mind.

Case Study

Decide what truly matters

Rachel, 50, divorced
Full-time, Self-employed, Business Owner
Self-imposed limitation: "I have to focus on surviving"
Courage practice needed: Live Your Values

The core issue

*"I feel like I just don't fit my skin anymore.
Is this really what I want to do?"*

Rachel was a successful self-employed business owner who came to coaching because she felt out of sorts. She described it as going from vibrancy and living in colour to black and white. Every day seemed the same, but more than this, the challenge of negotiating a divorce settlement meant she was stuck holding on to clients that paid well but left her feeling lacklustre.

Rachel was in survival mode. Each day felt the same and she was falling out of love with her business and life. Her strategy of moving forwards one step at a time enabled her to pay her bills but didn't provide fulfilment. It was becoming a job and that was why she had left employment 15 years earlier. Security mattered to her, but she felt deeply that something was missing.

Moving forward with little vision, and the recent divorce from her partner, was causing Rachel to feel like a machine going through the motions. When I asked Rachel the question, what was important about where she was, her answer was about financial stability for herself and her sons. A strong, capable woman, Rachel's heart yearned for something else. But what?

There was something about the fact that Rachel always wore black that struck me. It was such a harsh colour on her, and it felt like it was a uniform. When I asked her about it, she said she loved colours but had noticed she always went for the safe option of black. She described how it went with everything and looked professional, but she didn't feel good in it. That's when she told me that it was like a metaphor for how she felt, lost in the middle of her life, going through the motions.

When you're at a crossroads and the way forward isn't clear, you have an opportunity to connect to what matters. You can look back and remember moments that made you feel alive. In that remembering you feel the glimmers of aliveness that you felt at the time. That feeling of aliveness is information for you. It's a reminder. Where most people get stuck is they think they must recreate the exact situation again or that it was the external factors that created the feeling.

If all your choices come from being super-rational and logical, there is no heart in them. The path with heart matters, and if you're only using your logical brain to make choices in your life, you'll be missing your spirit and heart in your choices. It's only natural you feel something is missing, because you are only listening to one part of you.

It's like following a trail of aliveness and then noticing and being curious about what the common factor was underneath it. I find creativity helps to tap into a different way of thinking and knowing.

Rachel completed a creative exercise around her values. We explored peak and trough moments where she either felt alive or completely unfulfilled. She noticed that what brought her alive was adventures in nature, connecting with special people, and experiences where she was using her creativity.

From those moments we explored what values were in play and she identified six: **adventure, honesty, love, balance, connection, independence**. She then created a Pinterest board of her top 4 values and gathered photos and images that represented those values. The vibrancy and aliveness shone through her imagery. This gave her a sense of the energy she wanted in her life and was in stark contrast to the monochromatic professional image she had been holding herself to.

At our next session Rachel wore a beautiful bright magenta top. She described how she felt different. She was becoming conscious of how she had tuned out of her own frequency in favour of what she thought was a more reliable and dependable approach.

Rachel identified that she had been honouring a value of security. She had turned her work and life into a corporate job whereas she wanted it to be a colourful adventure.

She sat with an uncomfortable enquiry of what it would mean for her to be living in colour and she started to open to the idea that whilst she might be grieving the divorce and the life she thought she was going to have, a new possibility was arising.

When we let a new possibility in, we must let go of another reality. For Rachel that was letting go of her attachment to thinking she had to keep doing her business the way she had been doing it. She began to look at the clients she loved working with and from there she saw a new niche developing for her business.

As Rachel started to dream into this new possibility, she learnt to manage the inner fear that this new way of working would not be profitable or enable her to pay the bills. She practised self-trust and identified what supported her to hold an optimistic vision. She allowed herself to connect to her inner coach and manage the fear that would have her self-sabotage.

Understanding that her values could conflict gave her the insight to choose consciously. Instead of it being an internal battle where she began to doubt herself, she was able to recognise what was going on, separate out her fear-based thinking and decide whether to honour security or adventure. Rachel was empowered to act rather than react.

What Rachel learnt

That living a fulfilled life is a radical act and takes courage to actively prioritise her values and choose to live in colour. These values could guide decision-making when she was procrastinating. The only right decision was what felt viscerally right to her and aligned with her values. This resulted in Rachel finding a new passion for her business. She let go of associate work that was unfulfilling and started to craft her own message and community to work with clients that lit her up.

Courage Practice

Live Your Values

Every human being has emotional needs – to be safe and secure, belong and fulfilled. Your values provide the means to fulfil those needs and act as an inner compass guiding you through decision-making. To honour them you've got to make choices and take action to lead your life your way.

Become conscious of the decisions you make and how they link to your values so that you can consciously choose the focus of your attention. Check in with yourself at regular periods to see whether your actions are in alignment with what you say you value. If they're not you have the choice to recommit and take a different kind of action.

How to live your values

- Identify one value you want to prioritise in your life.
- Create a practice to help you focus on that value. It might be something visual or it could be that you set a reminder on your phone with the name of your value to message you at different points in your day.
- Check in at different points during your day and see how that value features in your decision-making process. Ask: what am I valuing here?

Ways to make this work

Decide what truly matters

- When you value many things, you don't really value anything.
- The hardest part of values work is actively deciding, prioritising and actioning your values.
- The prioritisation of your values may change during your lifetime. The key is to consciously prioritise and de-prioritise them according to your own knowing.

Audit — Four: Decide what truly matters

Accept

Accept

Build a healthy routine

DEFINE THE DIFFERENCES BETWEEN HEALTHY STRIVING, STRESS AND STRAIN

*The myth that women make better multi-taskers is not evidenced. It sets you up for unhealthy striving, trying to do and have it all. Learning to define your own rhythm will support you in your journey towards living your authentic life. The courage practice **Set Your Own Rhythm** will support you to take back control and know when you are at capacity.*

———————————

Are you striving for what you truly desire or what you think you should have to be accepted, approved of, be loved or feel significant? Do you find yourself pushing for some sense of achievement or satisfaction that comes and then dissipates, leaving you permanently seeking?

Healthy striving

Healthy striving is when you are clear on your intention, what that means for you and others and allow yourself to set your own pace and terms for success. I consider that 4 key areas underpin healthy striving:

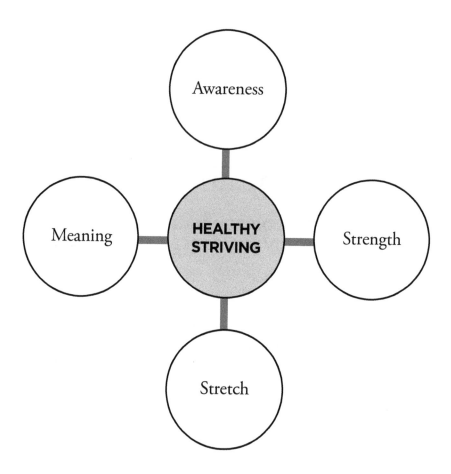

Awareness

Being aware of your reactive patterns (people-pleasing, controlling, conforming etc.) helps you know when you're running them and provides you the choice to change tack. When you are reactive you try to be something you're not – perfect, smarter, more likeable, quieter, louder. You are always trying to prove something to yourself, and there's an internal hustle to be seen, approved of and validated. Awareness gives you the choice to pivot your attention and focus on your unique strengths.

Strength

When you choose to play to your strengths you create an energy of positivity, productivity and ease within you. This creates flow and makes the stretch and achievement enjoyable.

Stretch

Eustress is a positive form of stress that benefits your health, motivation, performance and well-being. At work it might mean taking on a challenging project in an area you have experience and strength. At home it might look like setting yourself a challenge to increase your physical strength or setting a goal within an area that you feel passionate about. Finding your level of stretch will help channel your motivation and increase positivity and fulfilment.

Meaning

Without meaning, tasks feel monotonous and automated. Identifying why you do what you do will help you to know that even in the mundaneness or routine aspects of work and life there is purpose. The question to ask yourself when you're doing is, "For the sake of what am I doing this?" Connect to the deeper meaning that work and life give you and the impact and legacy you want to leave on others.

When you have healthy striving, you are clear on your intention – what drives you and gives you meaning. You play to your strengths, are aware of your emotions and conditioning and can stretch yourself to achieve the results you want without straining.

Defining healthy striving is an individual journey that requires you to know yourself. It requires observation, reflection, awareness, choice, and accountability.

When you unconsciously strive to be good enough, to be accepted and achieve, it's like a constant, relentless internal pressure to achieve. To transcend this pattern requires a move beyond the desire to please and be a good girl. You must define your own success criteria and benchmarks.

Conditioning and the relationship to striving

Your conditioning has a big impact on your striving practices. Let me be clear here, this isn't about blaming your parents, upbringing or culture. It is however about being willing to notice the environment that you've been raised in and understanding how that has shaped you.

For example, here's how I learnt to hustle and strive. I left home with an expectation and assumption that independence, knowledge and strength were key. Emotions were pushed down and covered with an attitude of "pull yourself together". Hard work, grit and determination were valued as was education which was seen as the way to get ahead and improve your position in life. The belief was that failure should serve to push harder. Achievement was rewarded with pride and love being expressed. I had learnt the behaviour of pushing and this had suppressed my inner knowing, intuition and empathy.

I, like all human beings, love the feeling of being loved and belonging. As a child I bundled achievement together with love. I had a limiting belief: I needed to prove myself because I associated achievement with praise and love. What was missing for me was my innate sense of worthiness. I looked for it on the outside, and the thing was, no matter what achievements I made, it never felt enough. There was always another training, another qualification, another step to take to climb and succeed.

There was always someone else doing or being better than I was. Comparison really was my thief of joy and the rise of social media and living in the midst of the competitive materialism of a leafy suburb of London only served to increase the sense of failing and needing to strive harder.

You are not me. My shaping will not be yours but there are some things that as women we have in common. Here are some of the comments I still hear women saying that fuel unhealthy striving patterns:

"My opinion is often talked over; I am often ignored and expected to do more menial tasks"
"I have to juggle a harder work-life balance"
"I have to work twice as hard as the men"
"I'm either a bitch or a doormat"
"People joke about who I had to sleep with to get here"

"I'm labelled as emotional"

"My opinion is ignored whilst my male counterpart can say the same thing and be heard"

"To get on here I have to behave like a man because I'm the only woman"

I am sure you have your own reality about what it's been like for you to be a working woman. I hope that these quotations do not reflect your own experience, yet I suspect somewhere along your journey you've encountered micro-aggressions that have made you feel you need to hustle for your seat at the table.

Hopefully this world of work is changing, and my intention isn't to depress you. I want to empower you. I want you to be honest about what underlies your unhealthy striving and inspire you to change that, should you wish to.

What won't work is being stuck and resigned to unhealthy striving practices whilst wishing it was different. That will just lead you to the path of doubt and resentment and you deserve more than that.

It is your birthright to live a life that honours who you authentically are, lights you up and sustains you. Just thinking that probably feels like a radical act. It is. You've probably got a host of limiting beliefs rising to your surface: money doesn't grow on trees, love won't pay the bills, creativity won't make money, I've got a mortgage to pay, my kids are expensive… I get it.

I thought all that too but what I've learnt is that unexamined beliefs are what drive unhealthy striving behaviours. The key is to hold them up to the light and *question if you believe them to be true or if you were just taught to believe them*. That's where your freedom lies.

Becoming conscious about my own unhealthy striving patterns gave me clues as to when I was heading towards overwhelm and burnout. I would feel my body tighten, my mind would race with lists of things to do, and I would become increasingly short-tempered and irritable.

It was not a wise use of my resources or power and it sure as hell wasn't enjoyable or fun, for me and those around me. My thinking wasn't supportive of how I wanted to feel; it was taking me deeper into the hustle for worthiness. I had to retrain myself to pause and pivot.

I also had to stop comparing myself to everyone else and the lanes they had chosen for their lives. I had to be clear with myself that I set my own limits and expectations, and that only I could hold myself accountable to them.

If you're starting to think you might have unhealthy striving, I have your back. As you journey through this book, you'll be able to dive deeper and discern what's next for you.

Define your healthy vs unhealthy striving habits

Before I move on, here's a checklist of thoughts, feelings and behaviours that may underpin unhealthy striving habits. Read through them and tick the ones that apply to you. Total up your healthy and unhealthy striving habit ticks.

If none of them apply, reflect and make a note of your own thoughts, feelings and behaviours that derail and support your striving habits. Ultimately, to make healthy progress towards what you want, your beliefs, thoughts, actions and behaviours need to be in alignment.

There are two tick columns on this list. One is for you to complete now, reflecting your current state of mind. The other is there to give you the opportunity to revisit this exercise in, say, one year's time and to see whether/ how far you have moved forward in your habits relating to striving.

Unhealthy striving habits

	Date (now)	Date (future)
Thoughts you may think		
My job is constantly demanding with deadlines which mean I can't put myself first		
It's easier to just do it myself		
My needs are less important than others		
If I can just get through this period, then it will be ok		
I need to prove myself		
If I achieve this, then I will feel better		
Others need help more than me		
Feelings you might experience		
Overwhelm		
Tired, exhausted		
Just a bit 'meh'		
Guilt about putting yourself first		
Resentful of others that do put themselves first		
Envy		

	Date (now)	Date (future)
Apathy		
Rebellious if you want to do things differently to others		
Behaviours you may do		
Put everyone else first even including the pet		
Avoid expressing your opinion		
Say yes when you mean no		
Not tell people when they cross a line with you		
Take everything personally		
Self-criticise		
Ticks sub-total		

Healthy striving habits

	Date (now)	Date (future)
Thoughts you may think		
I choose where and when I expend my energy and time		
Together is better – it is a strength to collaborate and ask for help		
I know myself and my capacity		
I am worthy of a happy, healthy life		
To bring the best of myself to every situation I need to prioritise myself		
I have innate gifts and strengths		
I set my own limits – I am constantly learning and growing		
Feelings you might experience		
Calm		
Presence		
Joy/excitement		
Fulfilment		
Acceptance		
Peace		

	Date (now)	Date (future)
Alignment		
Ease		
Challenge		
Behaviours you may do		
Prioritise your unique self-care practices to support being at your best		
Say how you feel and what you need		
Say no without justifying or negative 'what if'-ing		
Tell people when they cross a line with you		
Hold yourself and others accountable		
Self-affirm – validate your own value		
Ticks sub-total		

Reflection

Do the unhealthy striving ticks outnumber the healthy ones? If so, this really does need to be an area to focus on. Diarise a date, say one year from now, to revisit this exercise, redo it using the second column, and see how the tick numbers compare. Looking through the checklist, also ask yourself:

what other thoughts, feelings and behaviours trigger you to hustle for your worthiness? Jot them down here:

_____

_____

_____

Mood is everything

How you live your life and the mood you live in makes a huge difference to your confidence and how you feel. If you live in a mood of lack, stress and anxiety, you will find it hard to be open to new opportunities and step out. You will feel depleted and tired even on waking after sleeping.

One of the things I like to do is a mood weather check-in. I find that by doing this I take responsibility for how I am feeling and how I set my day up according to my energy.

This is how I do my morning check-in:

1. I take a couple of deep and centring breaths.
2. I check in with my body and how it feels.
3. I ask myself, "What is the weather in my internal system today?"
4. I name it.
5. I think about how I want to meet this energy.
6. I consider what I need and how this will impact on my top 3 priorities for the day.

Now, there are many times when I wake up with an intention to do this but something crashes into my day first. It might be the doorbell, my children, the dog or something else. I will find that I start days like this and I immediately feel like I'm trying to catch up with myself.

The agreement that I have in these moments is that instead of writing off the day because of its rough start, I can choose to slow down and start again. It takes courage to reset and begin again but I've learnt that it's better than pushing through regardless.

One of my clients undertook a variation of this practice. They would cycle into work, leave their bike in the office basement, and then take the lift to their workplace. During the lift journey they would check in and give themselves a score out of 10 as to how they were feeling. If they weren't at a 10, they would take the lift back down and walk around the block. They would consciously dial up a 10 and return to work.

You won't always be a 10 and your weather won't always be sunny. Some days your body is tired, and your mind is drained. The quality of your sleep will have impacted the way you feel. You don't need to feel guilty for not firing on all cylinders, but it is information into your system.

On days when you feel like this, it's important to re-evaluate and adjust your expectations. You may fail to do this and just push through, only to make mistakes and beat yourself up for failing to deliver on your expectations. Letting go of expectations but having an abundant expectancy is different. You are not attached to driving outcomes in the same way but are open to exploring the possibilities along the way.

Structure your day in cycles

Ernest Rossi was a psychologist who researched and wrote about ultradian rhythms. He advised that there is a natural rhythm of activity and rest that runs for about an hour and a half throughout our day. It's a rhythm because it takes place many times a day, which is what 'ultradian' means.[2]

He highlighted a new way of understanding stress, describing it as nature's signal that we are getting too high on stress hormones and need to take a healing break. He stated that most human error is due to fatigue and cited disasters such as Chernobyl as examples of this.

He noted that Leonardo da Vinci and Thomas Edison's best inspirations came after they had made a great conscious effort to solve a problem and then taken a break when they were initially frustrated with failure. After the break a new creative idea would pop into their conscious minds.

He described the tragedy of our society that we don't get enough rest and we try to stimulate ourselves artificially with drugs. In each workday most people can expect to experience 4 or 5 peak periods when they're at their best. The aim is to recognise your rhythms and work smarter, which is contrary to the presenteeism that often pervades our working cultures.

Rossi advocated taking a 20-minute break every couple of hours. This allows the 'Mindbody' to catch up with itself, reset and create the ideas and energy needed for the next chunk of work. He recommended that meetings should be for 90 minutes at most because otherwise people will get tired and be prone to error-making and frustration.

Accepting that you are an energetic being that doesn't have an infinite amount of energy gives you a responsibility to yourself. Instead of others defining the rhythm and structure of your day, you can empower yourself to set your own rhythm.

Now, if your critic is arguing how this is ridiculous, that there are either too many jobs in your day or that your boss would have a meltdown if you got up and exercised every 90 minutes, I hear you. But I'm not talking about extremes. You are designed for sprints at work, not ultramarathons. This means designing your priorities and work tasks so that there is variety such as different thinking and relationship opportunities. If you set a timer for 90 minutes you will be amazed how much you can get done. Once complete, you can reset, stretch, drink some water, and then choose a different activity.

Be intentional with your energy

It is incredible to me how many clients describe cultures in the workplace of back-to-back meetings with no real outcomes met as a result. They describe poor etiquette, noisy conversations, and agendas that are boring and don't address the real issues.

There must be a purpose to our conversations and meetings. The purpose may be to think through a dilemma by tapping into different viewpoints. Or it might be to connect and be in relationship with each other. Without purpose and intention, meetings are talking places where opinions get exchanged but true thinking and connection is not done.

Your own leadership with yourself requires you to take charge of your time and your energy. Know where you are in your energy, resource yourself and choose where and how you expend your energy. You will be amazed how much choice you have when you take charge and lead.

Habits that nourish	Habits that drain
Working in 90-minute sprints	Sitting at a desk for long periods
Drinking water	Drinking stimulants
Breathing deeply	Listening to gossip
Moving regularly	Meetings without clarity and purpose
Being aware of your daily top 3 priorities	Eating sugar and fast foods
Limiting interruptions and social media	Watching the news
Acknowledging what went well	Focusing on what is not working

Now identify your own habits that nourish and drain you:

Habits that nourish

_____

_____

_____

_____

Habits that drain

_____

_____

_____

_____

Build a healthy routine

> Rose, mid 40s, married, two children
> Part-time, GP
> Self-imposed limitation: "There's nothing I can do, it's the NHS"
> Courage practice needed: Set Your Own Rhythm

The core issue

> *"I feel stuck and powerless. I used to love what I do, now I just feel hopeless and trapped..."*

Rose's work as a GP was demanding in ways that she found hard to describe. Everyone knew how the NHS was underfunded and overwhelmed but that didn't stop patients complaining when their needs weren't met. Rose had chosen medicine as a profession because she wanted to care for people. She had observed her father's health problems and the help he relied on from his doctors and nurses and that had inspired her to go into medicine.

But Rose's dream of helping patients was waning. Her practice felt more like a time and motion study than it did a place to connect and support patients. She understood the business need in running an effective practice, but she was driven by her heart. The most heart-breaking aspect for her was that many of the conditions she was seeing were chronic and required patients to take responsibility and make changes to support themselves.

The old doctor-patient model no longer worked but the cultural myth still existed that GPs could fix all their patients' ailments. Rose had two young children and she was contracted to work part-time hours but, between the patient demands and the administration, she was always running late and working overtime.

She was frequently late to pick up her children from nursery and school and was paying more than she could afford on after-hours clubs. Her husband was frustrated by her constant complaining and exhaustion. She had grown increasingly irritable and short-tempered, and it was affecting their relationship. She felt like she was getting by and not really doing anything well.

When Rose shared her story with me, I felt like she'd put down a great big heavy monkey and expected me to pick it up for her. She wanted solutions from me. Of course, I had none because my role as her coach was to partner her to find her own inner resourcefulness and solutions. She gave me one example after another as if she needed to justify the insanity and unsustainability of it all.

I felt empathy for her frustration and powerlessness. Her situation felt deeply painful to me. But it wasn't my pain, it was hers. As her coach my job was to hold up a mirror, help her look at the reflection and then decide what to do next.

It is common in situations like this for clients to present a polarised perspective of their world. In Rose's case her conclusion was she either had to quit or put up with it. Rose was stuck. Neither option felt right for her.

Firstly, she had to get control of her emotional state. Currently she was overwhelmed, anxious and frustrated. When I asked Rose how she felt, the only emotion she could describe was frustrated.

Frustration was a reaction to her perceived lack of influence. She wanted things to be different to how they were. But to change it she first had to accept how it was. That meant meeting and softening into the frustration. She'd got used to speaking her frustration rather than feeling it. She complained a lot and each complaint only served to increase the frustration level.

Rose met this frustration by eating processed food and having a glass of wine to relax her in the evening.

"How does this work for you?" I asked.
"It doesn't," Rose replied.
"What makes you keep doing it?" I asked.
"Habit," she replied.

The thing about autopilot is that we operate without thinking. Have you ever driven somewhere and thought to yourself, *I don't remember how I got here?* That's autopilot. Rose's autopilot had her emotionally numb. She would recognise what she'd done afterwards but at the time her first instinct was to reach for a glass of wine or unhealthy foods.

To make any kind of change you must make the unconscious conscious. In Rose's case that involved creating a pause where she slowed down, felt the tension in her body and surrendered to it. We did this through a simple breathing exercise. With just 5 minutes of breathing, she felt calm. She could then be emotionally honest with herself about her frustration that was holding her back from moving forwards.

From a calm place she was able to accept that the circumstances around her were not going to change and the way that she was working wasn't working for her. Her GP practice would not suddenly magic up more time for her consultations, the patients weren't going to decrease, and her husband wasn't going to step in and rescue her.

But with acceptance of that reality, she could choose to empower herself. She could discern where she had influence and make changes. Rose was able to redefine her terms for success and address her boundary issues whilst also growing some interpersonal and leadership skills.

Up until this point her unhealthy striving had been driving her forward without questioning on a relentless treadmill that she couldn't get off. Once she accepted that all the power was going into a story about how she had no power, she was able to redefine her expectations of herself. She was able to answer for herself how she wanted to meet this oversubscribed, under-resourced system.

She decided that she no longer wanted to feel frustrated, exhausted and irritable. She wanted to take her power back and have command over how she expended her time and energy. From this place she stepped into her leadership and created a rhythm in her work that worked both for the practice and herself.

She decided to stop wasting her energy on worries and frustrations she could not solve, and she empowered herself to make the difference she knew she could make. She changed the structure and style of the conversations she had with patients. She began to explore their own motivations and choices around their health behaviours, and this helped to reduce unnecessary repeat visits.

Fundamentally she decided to stay; she picked her own lane and determined how she was going to operate within it. She stopped hiding in victim consciousness, blame and compulsive behaviours.

What Rose learnt

That her emotional habit was to run a pattern of frustration and then to numb the feeling of powerlessness that this generated. By focusing on where she had influence she stopped worrying about the wider concerns of the NHS that she had no control over and focused on how she could bring more effectiveness into her consultations. She practiced being clear with her boundaries and stopped wasting energy feeling guilty and wishing things were different. By focusing on her own self-care she created strategies to help her feel good and this boosted her own resilience.

Courage Practice

Set Your Own Rhythm

To examine your life requires curiosity for what has up until now been blindly accepted through your shaping. This isn't an easy practice but a necessary one because it enables you to understand how you've been working and living, why you've become so accustomed to it, and create the potential for you to make different choices to support you in living a happier, healthier life.

When you move to the beat of someone else's drum you are not at home within your sovereignty.

You need to manage your own energy system. You set the pace. You decide the rhythm. You can vary that rhythm when needed.

There will always be parameters set by the organisations you work for but often you have more agency than you think. Holding a focus on the outcome is important but there are many ways to reach desired outcomes and, unless you are micro-managed and have no task autonomy, you probably don't need approval to vary your focus and attention.

How to set your own rhythm

- Reflect on the rhythms in your day. Decide what cycles and rhythms you want between work, rest, renewal and play.
- Decide what matters and why.
- Decide where your limits are and what signals that you are at capacity or have reached an upper or lower limit.
- Stay in control.

Ways to make this work

Build a healthy routine

- Set yourself up for success.
- Presenteeism is not an effective way of working.
- Don't wait for permission to structure your work and rest cycles to support your productivity and well-being.
- Don't believe the story in your head that tells you it's not possible to structure your time and work cycles differently. Choose to empower yourself.

Embrace your own authority

OVERCOME APOLOGETIC ENERGY

*You are not an apology, you are an authority in yourself, what you like, how you want to set your work and life up to support you and your relationships. The courage practice to **Rule Your World** will give you agency and permission to approve of yourself and rise in your own life and work.*

———————————

You have many parts within you that are aspects of your sub-personalities. Some may be more known than others. Often the inner critic, worrier or doubter is the loudest voice within you. It provides a constant narrative of events in terms of what you should do, how you ought to act, what you would have done differently if you'd known better and what you could do if only you were smarter.

Accepting all your parts provides an opportunity to master yourself and consciously choose to lead with clarity and intention. It may be disconcerting to think about parts of you and their voices in your head but these secondary identities and parts of you make up your wholeness.

Your inner parts have good intention. As an example, an inner warrior may want you to move forward with heart and courage whilst an inner worrier wants to protect you by thinking through all the ways you may be rejected or abandoned. Both of their intentions are positive, but their impact might have the opposite effect to what you consciously want. Therefore, it's important to get into relationship with your many parts and choose which ones will support you to move forward authentically in your life. You get to turn the volume knob on these internal parts and decide what part needs to be loudest when you're stepping outside your comfort zone.

Create the right relationship within yourself

Perhaps it's the first time you've thought about this or maybe you've been living with parts of you but resisting conversation with them. When you resist, that part of you can run behavioural patterns under the surface. They may be fierce and courageous, nurturing, critical or bullying in nature.

I like to think of your inner selves like Russian dolls. You have many parts nested within you and your job is to find out who they are and what they need. You can do this by noticing when your inner dialogue is loud and asking, "Which part of me is speaking right now?" This will help you to connect with them, listen and ultimately manage and use them consciously as you journey through life.

You can notice how loud their voices are, when they show up and you start to work with them. This allows their wisdom to be heard, helping you to consciously choose to let your adult, powerful and resourceful self to be in charge.

You will have many selves within you, some of which are more familiar than others. For example, the wounded child, the good girl, the victim, the inner champion, the critic, the catastrophiser may well be ones that you know but there will be others that you haven't acknowledged. Being aware of your many selves gives you the freedom to be with them and choose how you respond to them.

Examples of inner selves

The good girl

The good girl wants to belong, be loved and feel safe. She is the part of you that will do things to please others or to fit in. You might notice the good girl is in charge by the following:

- Trying to do everything right
- Trying to be all things to all people
- Adapting to everyone else's needs
- Subjugating your own feelings and needs
- Waiting for permission

The shy girl

This is the part of you that's scared to be seen.

You might notice the shy girl is in charge by the following:

- Venturing to speak up but shutting yourself down
- Holding back your intuition and strengths
- Fearing you're too much
- Hanging back ,waiting for others to step in and go first

The catastrophiser

This is the part of you that imagines the worst possible outcomes.

You might notice the catastrophiser is in charge by the following:

- Constant 'what if' thinking
- Imagining the worst possible outcomes

- Fearing you'll be rejected, alone, unloved
- Feeling paralysed

The imposter

This is the part of you that believes you're faking it and will be found out.

You might notice the imposter is in charge by the following:

- Comparing yourself unfavourably to others
- Second guessing yourself
- Focusing on what you don't know whilst imagining everyone else knows more
- Present to your weaknesses as opposed to your strengths

Your wise self

This is the part of you that knows and trusts deeply in her knowing. She is the intuitive part of you.

You will notice that your wise self is in charge if you're doing the following:

- Focusing on your strengths
- Conscious of your feelings and needs
- Feeling resourced and confident
- Listening to your intuition and wisdom

The inner critic

Whether you call it a critic, gremlin or chimp, this part of you has you limit and criticise yourself. We all have one and it gives you a hard time.

You might notice the critic is in charge by the following:

- If your language includes the following: should, could, would or ought
- If you're criticising yourself
- If you're shaming yourself

Manage your inner critic

Remember in my survey how 93% of respondents said they were self-critical? It's this part of you that you want to get into relationship with, witness the fear and judgment it feels and then learn to get some distance from it.

Your inner critic will chatter incessantly in your head, particularly when you're at the edge of your comfort zone. It's the part of you that sabotages your happiness after you've had a great evening out and says, are you sure you weren't too much? It's the part of you that worries and judges and keeps you stuck in procrastination.

Yet it's the part of you that you probably rarely talk about with others. You think to yourself, is it just me, am I the only one that has this constant critical voice? You're not. In development workshops with women there is an incredible healing when we bring out the inner critics to the light. We give them a form by drawing them and writing down the things they say.

One by one women share phrases that their internal critic uses with them: "Who do you think you are?", "You're too much", "You're not enough", "You look ridiculous", "You're too old" and "You're too young". Everyone has their own set of things their critic says and they're in awe when they look at these other brilliant women sharing their vulnerability around their own critical voice. They realise they're not alone and it is part of the shared human experience.

They become aware that the image of confidence that they think other women present to the world does not reflect the magnitude of what they're holding inside. They break through the illusion of perfected ideals and discover a common humanity.

Getting into a relationship with your critic and personifying it helps you to separate it from the other parts of you. From this place you can choose how you manage this part of you. Some people give it a name because that helps create distance. Others draw it.

Having separated it you can then decide how you want to be with it when it shows up. You may choose to demote it or let it be a back seat driver in your car. You may choose to give it a different job to do like counting your breath. You may choose to instruct it to go away. Or you may turn towards it, listen, and then soothe it with another part of your more knowing and trusting self.

The key is to accept that it won't go away, particularly if you are claiming a more authentic life. It will always be with you and your job is to manage it so that it doesn't run your life for you. One way is to notice what triggers it. For some people the critic is so loud that they think that's the only part of them. Once you identify your critic and what it says to you, you have the choice to turn its volume down so that you can hear the other more resourceful parts of you.

In my own life I notice that my critic got triggered when people started to tell me what to do. My critic would come up and say, "They think you're stupid. You're coming across as thick. You should put them in line." It meant that I would react hotly to being told. What I began to see was that this developed from an authoritarian education accompanied by an unhealthy amount of elder sibling sarcasm.

My strategy for my critic is to notice it and then consciously soothe it by reminding myself that I am enough as I am. I found telling it to get lost didn't serve me. It made it louder. But knowing that authority triggered it helped me to understand my reactions and choose to respond with my own authority instead of emotional reaction.

The way you view and are in relationship with yourself matters. There were many comments in my survey that highlighted women giving themselves an incredibly hard time. Whether they perceived it as down to their upbringing, a refusal to be selfish, a lack of confidence or self-doubt, these women were caught in a self-defeating cycle.

It may be that you need to give yourself permission to do this work. Perhaps you think it's self-indulgent or you don't have time for it. Whatever you think you will find yourself right. It's what humans tend to do. But self-discovery leads to increased awareness and that in turn results in acceptance. Your critic, like the other aspects of you, is a part of you. Peace comes when you accept your nature and align the parts of you.

Leadership is not a title. It involves being clear, deciding what you want and committing to that decision. When you build your leadership on trying to satisfy others' expectations and desires, you don't put yourself in the centre of your own life and you are not leading. You are following the conditioned path.

Discover and embrace your inner authority

You are your own ruler and you either reign consciously or unconsciously. You have authority over your inner ecology: your thoughts, feelings, sensations, physical energy and spirit.

Perhaps, up until now, you have been unconscious of your inner ecology. When this happens, you move to the beat of the world and not your own internal rhythms. You ignore or suppress your own internal signals and voices in favour of listening to the outside world for how you should show up.

As your own ruler, you are always able to make a choice. You don't have to constantly react to the thoughts and feelings that your inner parts create. You choose which part of you is in the driver's seat.

When your doubter or inner critic is strong, as the ruler of your mental domain your authority decides how to preside over those voices. The same is true for your emotions. You are not a victim to your circumstances and emotions. You choose whether you ride your emotional waves, suppress them or defer them to your mental and ruminate on them.

Asking the question, "What am I aware of right now?" helps you to bring yourself into the present moment and see how you do rule your world.

- What are you aware of in your thoughts? If you step back and notice them as an observer, what parts are in dialogue? What is their language and intention? Are they trying to keep you safe or encouraging you to step out and lead?
- What are you aware of in your body? As you notice the body sensations, the places you feel and don't feel, the sensations that accompany your experience, you start to widen your lens and add more dimension to your current experience.
- What are you aware of in your emotions? Just being able to name an emotion is a huge release.
- What are you aware of in your spirit? Are you feeling expansive and aligned in your spirit or closed in and shut down?

As you start to create a picture of your own internal land you see patterns of behaviour and reaction. It's these patterns that give you choice.

Meet your inner authority

The following steps will take you on a journey to meet your own internal authority. I am indebted to my friend and colleague Gill Dore, as this process to help you to meet your inner authority was created in partnership with her.

The intention is to find harmony, and connect with the wise, sovereign part of you that rules your world from the inside out. So, there are no wrong or right answers here, simply ones that feel intuitively right for you.

Take some time to sit quietly with yourself. Sit comfortably and upright in your chair. Feel your feet on the ground and notice how beautifully you are supported without having to do anything at all.

Notice how it feels to be fully supported, physically and emotionally. From this place of feeling safe and held I would like you to imagine that you are about to meet your own internal authority, that part of you that holds your dreams, wants, actions and desires as priority and without question. It's the part of you that wants you to walk through the world in the way you were destined to do.

Now notice how it feels to be on the edge of meeting that part of yourself, with a curiosity and exploration that will bring you great awareness and clarity.

Make sure you are attending to your breathing. Remember that sense of safety – you are safe here in this moment. If you came here to fix yourself, let that go. There's nothing to prove or change. You are safe and you belong – just as you are.

This feeling is fully supported by your inner authority herself and with that sense of knowing let your imagination show you a beautiful mirror on the wall ahead of you.

You notice what the mirror looks like. It is big enough to see your head and shoulders although it may be a full-length mirror. It may be ornate or perhaps it's modern and simple; it may be colourful, gilded or studded with precious jewels. Whatever it is you imagine, firstly just look at your mirror and be aware of its size, shape and features.

This mirror can show you your inner authority, the self of you that wants you to lead your life and it holds your dreams, wants and goals as priorities above all else. In fact, your inner authority designed this mirror. She is proud and at peace with herself, as she knows the mirror doesn't just reflect back who you are outside but more importantly who you are truly inside. With unconditional love and without any filters. With that knowledge, notice if the mirror before you has changed in any way – remember, this is a visualisation so things may shift and change, that's perfectly normal.

In a moment you are going to stand up and look into the mirror and see yourself, remembering that you are safe and secure and that this mirror has its own authority and wants for you to be safe and well.

In your mind, now stand up and walk towards the mirror. Looking straight ahead, you see yourself coming into view, you can see your reflection… but it's different. This is now the reflection of your inner authority, the you who writes your own story in the world, the part of you who presides over your inner voices and is healthy, alive and sure.

Take a breath and look at her – what is she like?

What does she look like? It's you of course but how is she dressed? Take a moment to really see her. What does she represent through her image and external appearance? Is there anything that surprises you or, looking at this part of yourself, does she seem familiar?

What words would you use to describe her energy, her authority? What is she like when she steps forward into the world? Trust whatever words or images come to you.

When she steps forward into the world, with you, how does she talk? As the inner authority of your world how does she act and engage with people, problems and the world?

Take a breath and as you breathe in and out take in all that you know and continue to look at her. She is confident and comfortable with your gaze, she loves you.

Now consider, what does she bring to relationships that supports growth and love? What does she hold in relationships that maintains healthy boundaries for you? How does she respond when your boundaries are breached in relationships?

What does she welcome into the world for you? People, behaviours, ideas? What is it like to be in her presence when you are feeling alive and living fully to your sense of self and your desires?

What is not welcome? People, behaviours and ideas perhaps crowd in, and how does it feel to be in her presence when unwelcome events occur? How does she respond when negative or self-critical thoughts emerge?

Finally, if your inner authority were to hold a banner at a rally or event with a single message about what she stands for… what would it say?

Take your attention back to your breath and breathe in all that you know now about your inner authority. Keep your eyes looking at the mirror at your inner authority, reflect and take in all that you have learnt in this encounter and ask her one final question. What is her name?

It's a name or a title she is known by and relies upon. "I am xxx" – listen for and repeat the answer.

You both smile knowingly and as you turn to walk back to your chair you thank her, and she thanks you. As you return to your chair you notice a little gift, wrapped up and placed on the seat of the chair. You open it and sit with the gift in your hand.

This is a gift from your inner authority…

Notice the gift in your hand – what does she want you to know and remember?

Now, with your eyes closed, take three deep breaths and return to your current state, knowing that your inner authority is always there behind you, willing you forward. Her energy is always supporting you without you having to do anything at all. Her love is unconditional.

For an audio recording of this exercise, please visit: https://courageunfolding.com/resources/

The wholeness in your parts

When you're in a tight spot and one part is dominant and sabotaging your efforts, get outside of yourself and gain perspective by reminding yourself that this is just a part of you.

As I write this book, I notice my doubter self persists in coming up every time I get stuck or lack inspiration. Her intention is to keep me safe by having me abandon the idea of standing up as an author in my life. She fears rejection and ridicule and believes it's better to stay small and hide than stand out. She lives according to a limiting belief that "If I am too much, people won't like me". She asks me, "Who do you think you are to claim you're a writer?" Realising that she is one of many parts of me means that I choose to accept her presence and trust that the sage within me will guide me to write what I am passionate about and is informed by knowledge and lived experience.

Hold on to your power and sovereignty

There will be places where you follow but the one place you cannot follow is in directorship of your spirit and life. Only you know what is authentic and alive in you.

Leadership is a vulnerable choice. You don't know for certain when you step forward in your life and lead whether it is the right path. You don't know who you'll leave behind and whether new people will come into your life. Doubt and fear will accompany you.

Leadership is not simply related to work, it's about how you live your life each day with clarity, awareness and intention. You are responsible for how you want to show up in the world. Instead of going into situations hoping to find something, you become responsible for bringing what you expect to find. If you want a team to respect you, you bring self-respect. If you want a relationship to be loving, you bring self-love first. If you want a pay rise and you're being fobbed off, you decide whether to stay or move on.

Case Study

Embrace your own authority

Priya, 30s, married, two children
Full-time, Engineer
Self-imposed limitation: "Inner battle undermines confidence to act"
Courage practice needed: Rule Your World

The core issue

"I'm stuck and confused. One minute I want to go one way and another I think something different. It feels like I'm caught between different voices inside my head and locked in this strange battle..."

Priya was born into a culture where her parents wanted nothing more than for her to become a doctor. Education mattered to them, and it was perceived as the one way for girls to get ahead and succeed. As a child Priya dreamed of becoming an astronaut. She imagined flying off into space and seeing the world from a whole new perspective. But her dreams were shattered when she discovered that her eyesight would stop her from being any kind of pilot.

Medicine wasn't an option for her because she couldn't stand the sight of blood. Engineering felt like the next best thing, and she studied hard to excel in her class and be the first in her family to go to university. She graduated and began her career in a global technical company. She married and had two children and she had a great relationship with her husband who supported her ambitions. But there were aspects of her culture that made career progression difficult for her.

Her parents and friends felt that she should be happy with the balance in her life as it worked for them. But Priya felt something was missing. A part of her wanted to see if she could move into people management. She knew she got along with people well, but she was nervous of making a change.

She found herself stuck and unsure of what to do next. She was at a crossroads and whilst she had continually advanced her technical skills, she recognised that she had to move beyond being a technical expert. Should she accept where she was and the benefits that balance gave her, or should she step up the challenge level and apply for a people-management role?

Her issue was that every time she thought about making the move into people management, doubt crept in. She knew she was different to many techies in that she liked both the technical and the human relations side of work. But each time she thought about making the move she felt guilt about her family situation. Should she put them through this? What if she was wrong and it meant she could spend less time at home?

There was an inner battle going on inside her. One part of her was championing her like an angel on one shoulder telling her how capable she was, the other part was criticising her, the devil on the other shoulder pointing out her unreasonable expectations and delusions and all the ways it wouldn't work.

She found herself in a polarised conversation in her head. When her mood was up, she felt like she could make the move; when her mood was down, she was destined to stay in the same job forever. Priya was caught in this trap, and she felt like she must be the only person having this internal battle. This feeling of being the only one made her hide what was going on and pretend everything was fine.

When I asked what it was about being a people manager that attracted her, she came alive with resonance. She described how fascinating she found people and their behaviour. She talked of how she read books about psychology, privilege, and unconscious bias. She expressed a desire to create dream teams at work where people felt psychologically safe to dare to innovate, fail and learn.

No sooner had she expressed this dream than she turned to the other side and described how she loved her family life and didn't want to disrupt their balance.

Priya wanted me to tell her what she should do to get beyond this self-defeating cycle. She mapped out the mental thinking loop.

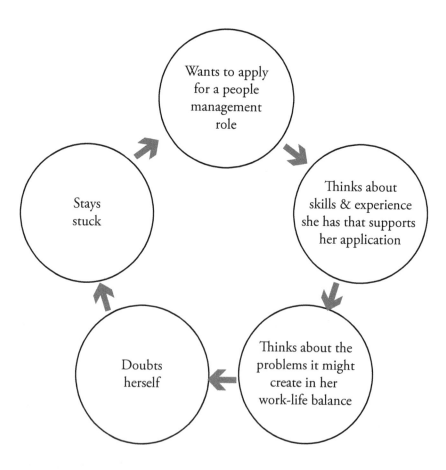

Priya was living inside a narrative that was creating doubt. It was a toxic conversation that she was having with herself, yet she had complete power over it.

Negative automatic thoughts were running her and whilst she began with the angel voice that championed her actions, the devil voice that pointed out what she lacked cancelled the affirming voice.

When you alter the quality of thoughts you change the energy pattern. We needed to release the stuck energy and find movement. Our job was to restore the person behind these thinking patterns.

To do this we explored Priya's inside team players, all of which had a purpose.

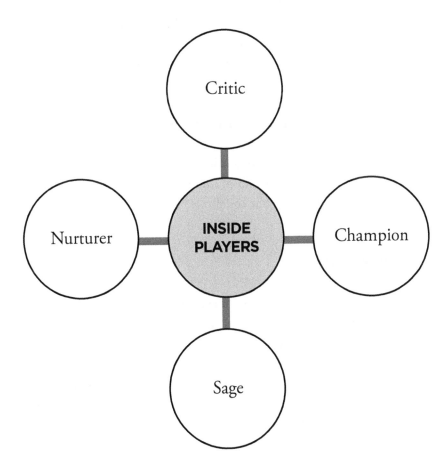

Priya identified that the champion was the first voice she often heard. It willed her on to be brave. It was this voice that had described the vision of creating psychologically safe workplaces and dream teams. Her critic was loudest when she started to step outside her comfort zone. It was a voice of impending doom that seemed to rob her of her dreams and conviction.

Her nurturer was a soothing, traditional, maternal voice that reminded her that things normally had a way of working out. Her sage was the quietest voice of all. It spoke when she was calm and centred, and whispered wisdom to her. This was the part of her that reminded her of her spirit and the value of being present in the moment rather than simply spending time in a role.

Accepting that Priya had these different parts that all had their own unique intentions helped her to understand what was creating the tension she felt. Instead of getting caught in feeling the weight of her fearful and limiting parts, she acknowledged their presence as a good thing because it meant that she was up to something big in her life. It helped to remind her that she was here for big things, not to play small.

Priya stopped entertaining the internal battle in her mind. She got to know herself in a totally different way, as ruler of her many parts. This involved seeing that she no longer had to give herself a hard time by engaging in a polarised conversation. She could soothe the doubting aspects of herself and remind herself that only she could rule her world from the inside.

What Priya learnt

That her first marriage was to herself and the many parts within her. She learnt to accept that there was no bad part and that listening to the internal voices that she had previously ignored gave her an internal peace and ability to consciously walk through fear towards her vision. As a result, Priya made the decision to move into people management and release the technical expertise that had kept her operating at the same level. She gained a promotion and began a new journey that played more to her natural strengths of empathy, positivity, creativity and strategic vision.

Rule Your World

There is a choice to be your own inner apology or authority. To move out of apology means claiming that you know yourself best. It takes practise to be in your own power and authority instead of acquiescing to others. Give yourself permission to claim your expertise, knowledge, skill, worthiness and unique essence. Make yourself a ruler of your own world and notice what it's like to lead from the inside out.

Watch when you give your power and authority away. Don't engage your inner critic to chastise you for defaulting to an old way of being. Instead, practise choosing to call your authority back.

How to rule your world

- Spend some time reflecting and journaling about how you want to rule your world.
- What are the terms of engagement for you in work and in your relationships?
- Think back to your values. What values must be honoured in your reign?
- What boundaries do you have for work and in relationship?
- What are you clear that you will say yes to and what you must say no to?

Ways to make this work

Embrace your inner authority

- There's an apologetic energy that accompanies the good girl syndrome.
- If you find yourself waiting for permission, holding back your opinion, apologising and seeking approval and affirmation, remind yourself to connect with your inner sovereign.
- Let her rise and rule because anything else is reaction to situations and people and not leadership in your own life.

Align

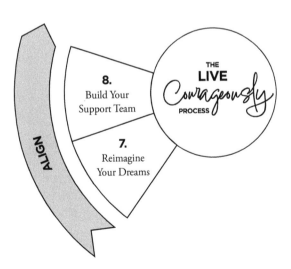

Align

Reimagine your dreams

LET GO OF DISAPPOINTMENT TO DREAM AGAIN

When you've lost faith, your heart feels broken and the vulnerability of knowing that you might never realise your dreams feels too great, you can lose yourself to your disappointments. The courage practice **Dare to Dream** *will support you in rediscovering your own dreaming again.*

Dreaming helps you get a sense of the essence and bigger picture of what wants to unfold in your future. Marrying this with identifying milestones and short-term goal-setting helps to break this down and direct your motivation so that you can sustain your efforts to realising those goals.

Wherever you are in your life journey, dreaming and goal setting can support you. The key message is that you can use dreaming to imagine a new reality and that whilst there might be a process to get you to the dreaming stage, everyone can dream. But what do you do when you're stuck in limbo because there's a dream that you haven't been able to make happen?

Grieve the disappointed dreams

When there is a disappointed dream there is also the opportunity to fall into a victim mindset. You feel it's not fair and you genuinely feel sorry for yourself. Perhaps you find that you've built something according to someone else's vision or dream. Whilst deeply confronting, the realisation also gives you conscious choice.

A common client example is from those that have invested building their career in a particular field only to find it lacklustre. They went into it because they were good at subjects at school and had been shaped by the advice from family and career advisors that it would be good for them.

But the reality turned out to be different, so they are confronting both the new information they have about what fulfils them in their career but also the disappointment and fear that this is not how they thought it would be. They have thoughts of regret, "if only I had done it earlier", but that thinking keeps them stuck in a cycle of regret and self-abandonment.

Whether they choose to stay in the career or dream a new dream, the choice is theirs. The key is to choose consciously.

Identifying that you have a disappointed dream helps you to release the emotion and move through to what wants to unfold next in your journey. It's when you unconsciously hold on to disappointment and harbour resentment that it keeps you stuck.

High and low dreams

Do you ever desperately hope for something to happen but play it down when others ask you about it? Do you sometimes long for an occasion to be special whilst telling people that you're not that bothered?

Dreams may or may not come true, but the dreaming is important for us to create an authentic and fulfilling vision and walk towards it. You can dream positively (a high dream) or negatively (a low dream).

The survey comments highlighted both high and low dreams. Examples included a desire for more self-care whilst also feeling guilty and imagining being a burden to others or a desire to prioritise their own needs but fearing others wouldn't love them if they did.

When you have these high and low dreams happening at the same time and you're not aware of them, you give off mixed signals to yourself. For example, you hope a presentation at work will go well. It matters to you and your team. You feel excited by the possibility but you're also aware that some of the key stakeholders are challenging so you play it down to others. Or you hope an anniversary will be special but describe it as "just another year" to your partner to avoid disappointment.

If you want change in your life, then becoming aware of the high and low dreams is a helpful part of the process. You can then choose consciously to commit to the high dream, set goals or milestones and take consistent action towards it.

In my own experience, I've often found that the high dream is easy for me. I'm a futurist in my thinking and I love to dream things into possibility. But the challenge for me has been a resistance to speak the low dream. An example can be found in my own development as I journey through self-employment. I have found myself holding back from investing in development programmes to build my visibility and grow my business because I have given credence to the low dream and allowed my inner critic, who wants to protect me from rejection and disappointment, to self-sabotage my efforts.

In writing this book I have been conscious of both the high and the low dream behind the scenes and have shared them with my mentor, Karen. There have been times when I've shown up to our sessions full of doubt, writing and rewriting sections, questioning if things make sense or if I'm deluded, and reluctant to share my progress with my community.

Having coach mentoring support during this journey has been incredibly helpful as a spur to break through and step up by being reminded that if I don't write it, I will have affirmed my low dream and will actually have helped and supported nobody to find their courage.

Karen has been the person that has helped me to take a stand for my high dream. I imagine that I've driven her crazy at times as I oscillate between my high and low dream. Each time I do this, she's held space for me and been an ally to help guide me back towards my high dream.

Being conscious of whether you're closer to your high or low dream helps you to explore why and what wants to happen. You can connect to your inner saboteur or critic in these moments, who is trying to protect you but is actually limiting your dreams.

Dream a new vision

There are many ways to dream, and you probably have a sense of what works for you. The starting point is to accept the nature of dreaming. It's a state where you're relaxed and at ease and able to tap into a different consciousness. There is no forcing in dreaming. It's not a place to push or squeeze your attention. It's a place of surrender and allowing.

You must develop an optimistic self-confidence with dreams. The goal is to allow yourself to become the dreamer. If your imagined future is better, it gives you hope. If your imagined future is worse, it gives you anxiety.

Ultimately, when you're with other people you're all dreaming each other up. You see an image of a person and you imagine who they are, what they value. The same is true of organisations. I have worked with women who have identified with a brand image of a company only to be disappointed when they're working inside the reality of it. The experience does not match their dream of it.

Being clear and conscious about your dreams gives you a chance to identify with your highest hopes and worst fears. That gives you the opportunity to take ownership and talk to others about your hopes and fears.

But the challenge is that dreaming is something that often gets knocked out of you as you grow and develop. As a child it's natural to dream and fantasise about who you will be when you grow up. Anything is possible until you hit school, when you learn harsh new truths. You may have been told that dreaming is for play and that creativity won't pay the bills. As a result, you become disconnected from your true desires, and base your dreams on the idea of what you think you can have in your conscious mind. Perceived practicality overrides what the heart wants.

Equally, you may find that you're impatient or perhaps feeling a bit desperate to dream. You may have a disappointed dream that you're still grieving and finding hard to release. But it's in the surrendering that something new eventually comes. To discover who and what you want to become, you must allow yourself to dream.

I remember distinctly how hard surrendering can be, but I learnt the lesson best through experiential learning. When I was 43, I decided to go to California as part of a 10-month leadership programme. I had quit my job and put my savings into this training. I felt I needed to squeeze every bit of value out of this training, and I was desperate to learn everything I could.

The training was surprising because it was primarily practical. I found myself completely freaked out, at my edge during one exercise on the high ropes course. I could feel everyone's fear as they listened to the instructions. I wanted to overcome my fears but at the same time I felt completely paralysed. The hardest exercise for me was the first one. We had to climb up a tree and then fall backwards and be caught by our fellow tribe members. The instruction was to imagine you were squeezing a penny in your butt cheeks and keep your hands straight by your sides. I had seen someone go before me and they hadn't kept their hands by their side. The impact was they caught someone in the face that was catching them.

I was terrified but not for the obvious reason. I didn't want to hurt someone, and I didn't know if I could trust myself to keep my hands by my side. The leader told me that I was in an old story, and it was time to step through. I cried, not knowing if I could do it. And then I took a deep breath and let go. I will never forget that feeling and the clarity of the decision that preceded it.

I was tired of holding myself back. I wanted to claim a new story and I consciously decided that this was nothing to do with the falling back and everything to do with building self-trust. I realised that I had to have my own back first and that the stories I made up about whether I could trust someone began with myself. Trust is a vulnerable choice and whilst I was high trust with other people, I was low trust with myself. I decided to change that, and I can still remember the visceral feeling of surrendering in that moment.

Dreaming is a similar place of surrendering. It is a vulnerable process. You must imagine that despite being where you are a new possibility is available. You must hold the tension between imagination and current reality. I know when I am in my darkest moments dreaming is something that I struggle with.

I have learnt that it requires self-trust. Part of my learning was accepting that as I moved through to the chapter after divorce, I wanted to create a comfortable, successful life for myself. I envisioned comfort by walking in beauty as well as believing myself worthy of success and joy.

Your dreams may come in metaphors and the meaning of them may unfold over time or you may hear specific words or statements. However you dream is right for you and there's something about allowing yourself to notice and play with what arises.

If you hold your dreams too tightly you try to become too literal about them. However, if you can explore the symbolism within them you will start to uncover new insight and meaning. Sometimes, in working with clients, they want to know what a symbol means, and they will look for meaning outside of themselves. What matters is what it means for you.

Dreaming for logical thinkers

If you're a logical thinker, you may prefer a structured dreaming process. The following exercise can help you do this.

Create a timeline of your life's milestones

One way to do this is to envision a new future by planning backwards. You can do this by creating a timeline for your life up to the age of 60 (anything after that is regarded as bonus time). If you're in your fifties this might freak you out because you have so many plans in your head that you haven't yet actioned. You may decide to choose a different date to imagine yourself at but if you have that feeling of having too much to do and not enough time, check in with what really matters.

- Imagine yourself at 60, older and wiser.
- Identify what the key milestones have been from your current age to you aged 60.
- If you have children, you might want to track their ages alongside your own to give a wider picture.

Take your time with this exercise and give yourself permission to dream and feel into the milestones.

If you're a visual learner, you may want to take this a step further and create a vision board or a vision movie. Humans move towards what they picture in their mind's eye, so the advantage of a vision board or movie is that it acts as a guiding light. This can help you picture your future and relax the grip on any current frustrations. The vision can then translate into tangible goals and meaningful action.

When I allowed myself permission to dream, I created a QuickTime movie. The movie was a collection of images that represented my milestones. Some were achievements like a ticket for a speaking event that I had held at Alternatives, or the cover of my book, but others were images of my values expressed in nature and service of others. The final picture was of Uma Thurman's character in the yellow jumpsuit from the movie *Kill Bill*. That image captured the kick-ass energy that I knew I needed to propel myself forward and make my vision reality.

Each day I would play that movie to myself, reminding myself who I was becoming and unfolding within myself. It helped me to stay focused particularly on down days. The key is to hold a vision whilst also being unattached to the outcomes. In other words, you picture it happening in your mind's eye whilst staying open to the opportunities that arise in the moment. It has taken me 6 years from creating that movie to finally giving myself permission to write the book that you are now reading.

There were many times when I had lost faith that it would happen, but something magical happens when you hold the possibility without being attached to the specific outcome. It's as if the divine timings go to work and when the space opens, you take aligned action towards the essence of that dream you've been holding. The milestones and timelines are guideposts that help build confidence and trust in where you are heading.

Dreaming for creative thinkers

If you're someone that prefers to imagine a possibility, the following guided visualisation will help you to connect with your conscious and subconscious mind. You may experience images, sounds, words and felt senses during the visualisation – trust what comes and if nothing comes that's ok too. The key is to be at ease and open yourself to the experience of what wants to unfold within you.

As with everything it's important to have clarity of your motive and intention with this work. Repeat the following statement to yourself:

*"My motive is love and harmony and I am going
on a journey to connect to my future self."*

- Close your eyes and take a moment to settle into your seat. Feel your feet on the ground and notice how beautifully you are supported without having to do anything. Notice the contact your body makes with the chair and how completely supported you are in this moment.
- Now turn your attention inside your body. Notice your breath without trying to change it. Just notice. Is it shallow and high up in your chest? Perhaps it's coming from deeper down in your belly. Just notice.
- As you breathe in and out, notice the temperature of cool air coming in through your nose or mouth and warmer air escaping on the exhale. Allow yourself to settle into your own rhythm for your breath. Allow any thoughts and tensions of the day to fall away. On the inhale silently say to yourself "let" and on the exhale "go". Continue for 3 further breaths.
- On your next inhale imagine that you are on a journey to your favourite place in nature. Look around you and notice what surrounds you. See the colours and shapes, textures, sounds and smells. Take this place in and allow it to rejuvenate your energy.
- In the distance you see a path. You walk towards it and make your way along it. The path is soft beneath your shoes, a mixture of bracken, fallen leaves and pine needles. As you walk, your body relaxes and your mind clears.
- You see a gate in the distance, and you head towards it. You notice a figure on the other side of the gate and as you move closer you see that it is your future self. This is you 10 years into the future when your needs and desires have been met.

- Take a moment to notice her.
- How does she stand?
- What clothes and colours is she wearing?
- What is your sense of her energy?
- In the field behind your future self is a beautiful, shaded bench. Its position provides just the right amount of warmth and freshness. You can smell the earth around you. Your future self greets you in her own special way and you move towards the bench for a conversation.
- Ask your future self:
  - What has unfolded in her life in the last 10 years? (Pause and listen for the answer.)
  - What does she love about where she is today? (Pause and listen for the answer.)
  - What brings her joy? (Pause and listen for the answer.)
  - What has helped her build her resilience and stay in her own well of being? (Pause and listen for the answer.)
  - Now ask her anything you intuitively want to. (Pause.)
- It's time to leave your future self but before you do, your future self has something she wants to give you that will remind you of who you are becoming. She gives you a treasure from nature and you take it in your hands and thank her. You explore the treasure and what it means to you.
- It's time to say goodbye in your own special way. You turn, walk back to the gate and set off back on the path to your place in nature. This is the place where you feel safe, and you can always return to at any time.
- You leave your place in nature and return to your body. Take in a few deep breaths, breathing in and breathing out. On your next inhale start to move your body, returning to the present moment and to the room you're in. And when you're ready, open your eyes and take a few moments to write down your observations.

For an audio recording of this exercise, please visit: https://courageunfolding.com/resources/

Whether you get specific information from this visualisation or not doesn't matter. It's about accepting that a future you exists and that you can tap into your imagination and connect with that part of you. You can continue to explore your relationship with your future self by asking at any point how she would act.

You are always becoming. You cannot not become. With clarity of intention and motive you can walk a path that is uniquely you. This can help you navigate turbulent times, trusting in your own resourcefulness and knowing. It creates a psychological safety within you that is not reliant on outside approval or validation.

How you hold your dreams matters. You, like me, have been conditioned to be goal orientated. It's how Western society works. Set a goal, work like crazy to achieve it, celebrate and then set another goal. As new evidence informs how we can maximise our human operating system it can feel conflicting, and the tendency can be to throw the baby out with the bath water in pursuit of the next best thing.

I have talked to you about visioning and goal-setting in this chapter and they are two very different processes, but they work well together. I used to find myself torn, walking an imaginary continuum between woo and spiritual teachings and pragmatic, evidence-based psychological tools. I have learnt that the medicine is inside all of us, and these tools and teachings can provide insight and understanding, guidance and support, but at the end of the day your belief system is exactly that, yours.

For me, I decided to take the best of the psychological tools that supported me and combine them with my shamanic beliefs, breathwork, yogic philosophies and practice. Finding what supports you to hold a dream and act in support of its realisation is key. Working with a coach provides someone neutral, outside of you and your dreams, who supports you and believes in your wholeness and resourcefulness. Creating an environment of high support and challenge provides a rich ecology and alchemy for growth to occur.

Case Study

Reimagine your dreams

Sarah, late 30s, married
Full time, Occupational Therapist
Self-imposed limitation: "It's supposed to be different to this"
Courage practice needed: Dare to Dream

The core issue

*"It wasn't meant to be like this. I thought my life
would turn out differently. Now what?"*

Sarah had gone through two unsuccessful rounds of IVF. She had always assumed that she would be a mother. As a child it was something she talked about with her friends. They would write the surnames of their latest boyfriends and think about what they might call their children. Whilst she was happy for her friends who were all getting pregnant and having babies, a part of her felt like it just wasn't fair. She found it hard to hold these different emotions inside her.

Sarah enjoyed her job as an occupational therapist. No client was the same and she still found the work humbling after many years. Her manager kept encouraging her to apply for a leadership position but with everything that had happened, Sarah felt heartbroken and unsure if this was the right path for her.

She had accepted that they were not going to go for another round of fertility treatment, but she found herself feeling increasingly sad and despondent.

She came to me for coaching because her world was getting smaller, and she wanted to change how she felt about the future. But the thing was, she couldn't imagine a different future. She had been so attached to how she thought it was going to be that she didn't know where to start. Sarah wanted to do and feel better, but she didn't know how. She couldn't decide whether to apply for a leadership role and felt like she was constantly doing mental gymnastics about the idea.

Sarah's first challenge was to let go of the dream of how she thought her life was going to turn out. She had dreamt a future with children, and it no longer looked like this was in the forecast for her. But as much as she wanted to let go, she was emotionally caught in disappointment.

Meeting Sarah where she was in her journey meant that she had to see the dream for what it was and how it had shaped her expectations of what would happen. Once it was named and identified as a high dream she was able to grieve it. It took time to process this, and she had to learn to turn towards herself with self-compassion instead of telling herself how she should pull herself together. Sarah began to acknowledge her hurt feelings and say compassionately to herself that it was natural for her to be grieving and that she was doing the best she could.

Allowing her feelings to rise, she learnt to process and ride them. They came in waves and the strangest of things would set them off. She would see an advert on TV or walk past a park or notice a family-sized pizza. Instead of suppressing these feelings, Sarah sat with them and repeated a mantra to herself: "*This too shall pass*".

With time Sarah started to notice that a space was evolving. She described it as being like a blank page with nothing written on it. She didn't yet know what she wanted to write on this new page, but she could feel her energy wasn't constantly being pulled into grief and as it lifted, she started to wonder about what the next chapter in her life might include.

She started to make small changes. She changed her hairstyle and wore more colours instead of the safe black, navy and grey. She joined a running group, having never run a day in her life before. She joined in cross-country trials and found herself having tea out of flasks and eating homemade cakes on cold, dreary days that would previously have been full of sadness.

She noticed how healing nature was and she loved being outside. Being in green spaces lifted her soul and she started to think about what it might be like to have a dog. She'd never had a dog growing up, but she'd always loved them. Fate took its course when a contact in the running club knew of someone that was looking to home a puppy. Despite all her reservations Sarah and her husband decided to give the puppy, Rufus, a home.

It amazed Sarah how different she felt. Her spare time was filled with nature and activity, and she found it joyful how many people stopped and talked to her and Rufus. Slowly she began to fall in love with her new life and she realised just how many of the simple things had been missing.

With time Sarah began to connect to her essence, vision and inspiration. As her life changed incrementally, she started to reflect differently on her career and this question of whether she should move into a leadership role. She was now aware of what sparked joy in her life and had realised her state of grief and disappointment.

She began to imagine how a leadership role would fit with her values as she grew more confident in this new life. Her courage unfolded and she decided not to apply for a vacant position that she was being encouraged to. She realised that stepping into leadership would have met other people's dreams for her but not her own.

She knew what balance she wanted in her life, and what she loved about her job. She made a conscious decision to deepen her skills as a specialist rather than taking on the traditional progression of moving into leadership.

She created a timeline for her life and with milestones that excited her. Sarah started to get a sense that her future self was free, brave, and adventurous.

Sarah used short-term goal-setting to help her maintain motivation and momentum towards the vision, but when things came up, she let go and adapted to them. She practised ease and healthy striving towards her vision.

Sarah completed the courage audit in Chapter 3 to explore the different aspects of her life. She then highlighted that the area she wanted to set some goals in was personal growth. In her career she lasered in and identified the areas within her field that she wanted to specialise in and the skills, knowledge and experience gaps that she had. She created some short-term goals that would take her towards deepening her knowledge over the year.

Sarah identified that she wanted to broaden her experience and sense of adventure. Life had got smaller in the time she had been focused on the IVF and she knew she wanted to have new adventures with Rufus. Together with her husband she bought a VW camper van and they set themselves challenges of travelling around the UK. They planned trips, dog walks and mini adventures that sat alongside her career goals.

What Sarah learnt

Relationships are frequently built on myths of how we think things are going to be. To move beyond her myth, she had to grieve its loss in her life. Between a beginning and an ending is a transition. It's where nothing makes sense and that's ok. It's not supposed to make sense; you must ride through it as best you can. Being gentle and kind to yourself in this period helps.

Sarah's ability to dream returned when she was feeling relaxed, with an open mind and heart. This resulted in Sarah recommitting to her work as an occupational therapist and choosing to honour her home life, personal relationship, and new fur baby.

Courage Practice

Dare to Dream

Dreaming happens when you're in a relaxed state and you've entered a state of surrender and possibility. If you're feeling like you must figure out what's next, it's going to be difficult to relax and tap into your subconscious. In these instances, you're better off to do something completely different like get out in nature so that you give yourself the self-care to centre and relax first.

How to dare to dream

- Practise grounding and journeying into your dream world.
- Always have a clear motivation and intention. For example, love and harmony to receive a message from my future self.
- Be open to discovering the medicine that's inside you.

Ways to make this work

Reimagine your dreams

- Dreams unfold over time and sometimes we cannot make sense of the steps in the journey to manifest them until we look back.
- Openness to the possibility and practising patience is key to manifestation. Your life is not a sprint, it's an ultramarathon.
- When you're in a dark place, you may have to borrow from someone else's belief – we will talk about that in the next chapter but for now allow yourself the gift of dreaming and patience.
- Trust that your soul is always calling to you and it knows what wants to unfold. Pay attention and listen to its calling.

Build your support team

LEAN INTO THOSE WITH CAPACITY

*Everyone at some point in their life needs lifting. As women we have been conditioned to be stoic, strong, independent and capable but the truth is, together is better. So, to help you lean into the right people without losing yourself or your resourcefulness, I've created the **Define Your Support Team** courage practice.*

Habit change requires persistence and consistency. Transformation happens in a culture of high support, challenge and positivity. Making a big change in your life or work will impact those around you. You may unintentionally create waves of confusion and fear. It's human to expect those closest to you to be your best advocates but when you changing creates a ripple effect on them, they may not be the best people for you to lean into to support you activating your potential.

Know who has capacity and for what

I invite you to think deeply about who is in your support team. Identifying who you go to, for what, and the effectiveness of that support, will ensure that you approach the right people at the right time.

Imagine that you want to ask for a salary increase. You believe you deserve it but you're not sure if it's the right thing to do. People around you say it's not the best time to ask and remind you that there's an upcoming recession and jobs may be less secure than they have been. They suggest you don't rock the boat.

There are many ways to explore this issue but being clear first on what the challenge is will help to identify what support is truly helpful. If you were supporting this person, what kind of support would best suit them? Is it emotional or cognitive?

The problem with advice is that it comes from someone else's frame of reference and ignores the other person's own resourcefulness. The decision can only be answered by the person in this scenario who feels they deserve a pay rise but are fearing the consequences of making that request.

Emotional support in this scenario might be to empathise with their experience, enquire what's getting in the way of them making their request and reminding them of their resourcefulness to handle whatever shows up.

In the past I've habitually reached out to people I think should get me: close family members, friends that know me. But talking to a friend about my business doesn't help me and talking to my mum about my fears may well trigger her own worries for me.

In my journey through my divorce and beyond I had several health challenges which impacted me on several levels. I noticed that friends wanted to spend time with me to offload their problems but didn't have capacity to talk through mine.

I spent a long time complaining, feeling victimised, that they didn't get me, until I realised that it wasn't their fault. They were being themselves and I was expecting something that wasn't possible from them because they didn't have the insight or capacity to truly help.

I found taking a structured approach to analysing what was going on in these dynamics helped to release the drama I was holding around this. I used an approach from Caitlin Walker and Marian Way to help me reflect and identify the core issues.[3]

The approach was simple. I reflected on the people that I got on with and identified what they did, what I inferred from that and the impact of those behaviours on me.

For example, when I was with one friend, they would only talk about themselves. I would infer there was no space for me, and the impact would be that I felt tired and ignored in their company. When times were hard, they would say things like "I'm sorry", I would feel patronised, and the impact was I felt like somehow I was doing life less well than they were.

In contrast to this, another friend would listen deeply and without judgement, and I would infer from this listening that it's ok to vent and express myself and the impact would be that I felt normal, human, and equal to them in my messiness.

From this analysis, I could identify that the values friends held impacted the relationship dynamics. Depth, authenticity and connection mattered to me and the people that needed to be in my emotional support team needed to share that value of depth.

It wasn't that I couldn't be with the other friends, but I could save myself the heartache of being with them and expecting them to be something they weren't. I could have boundaries about the things we talked about.

You need different types of support in the various areas of your life, so think about finding people who fit these characteristics:

- **Emotional support** – people you can go to, be vulnerable with and they won't try and fix, cajole, scold, or rescue you
- **Career/professional development support** – people with real expertise that can help you think about your career
- **Health/wellbeing support** – people who lift you and encourage you to be the best version of yourself
- **Financial support** – experts who can help you with financial planning
- **Business support** – experts in running their own business. These are people with a proven track record in sales and business management

Discover your emotional support team

When you think about your emotional support team you want to think less about what people do or the skills that they have but more the way that they make you feel. A fundamental skill someone needs to have to emotionally support you is the ability to listen, fully and without judgement.

Characteristics and impact of being with people that make me feel safe:

- A clear, strong opinion
- Self-expressed – articulate their feelings
- Clarity of desire – not a constant guessing game
- Hold different perspectives – not judgemental
- Get beyond blame
- I feel like I exhale in their company
- They demonstrate empathy not sympathy

What they do	What they don't do
Patience	Repeated phone calls, texts
Aware of the emotional environment they're in	Overcommunicate or talk over you
Clarity	Ask what's wrong with you when they sense something
Directness of conversation	Me syndrome – dump emotionally
Express emotions clearly	Eye-rolling
Listen	Insensitivity to feelings
Ask	Neediness or victim energy

Now define your own characteristics for who makes you feel safe in your relationship with them.

What they do

_____

_____

_____

_____

_____

What they don't do

_____

_____

_____

_____

_____

_____

What I identified with this list was that I needed to stop going to people that didn't have the capacity to hold me in my emotions and vulnerability and then making them wrong because of their incapacity. I had to create a new support team. I decided that I was worthy of being comforted and supported.

Know your relationship red flags

A good way to reflect on this is to journal some of your interactions with friends and colleagues. This needs to be raw self-reflection in how you interact as a support to others, and how honest and authentic you are. Here are some questions to pose to yourself:

- Do you tiptoe around someone?
- Do you lose your autonomy and decisiveness when you're with someone?
- Are you masking your authenticity with someone?
- Are you feeling like you must change yourself to be with someone?

- Do you lose a part of yourself in relationship with others?
- Do you find whenever you talk about yourself and your needs, they switch the subject to themselves?

If you adapt and shapeshift to stay connected to people, it's important to ask if this is serving your authenticity. If someone puts you down, it doesn't matter whether it's a boss or a lover, it will have a negative impact on you.

People who care about you know who you are. They know what makes you come alive and what causes you to shrink. Through being in toxic environments, I realised that a part of me had accepted this was just the way it was and that I needed to be better. But the thing is that all the responsibility for creating the right relationship was on me.

This insight helped me to slow down and identify that a lack of authenticity and honesty was a big red flag for me. For many years I tried to swallow and subjugate my needs, but I realised I needed to create a new story, stop abandoning myself, and speak my truth.

Identifying your red flags will help you to be intentional in your relationships and avoid the trap of being with people who don't support your authenticity and courage.

Make clear requests

Complaints are a turnoff for most people. Whether you're a manager listening to complaints from your team or a mother listening to how unfair life is for your child, it's not much fun to listen to. But for the complainer it's worse because every time they repeat the story and the complaint, they re-experience the emotion of it. This is how resentments get built and they reinforce a critical mindset.

A complainer is seeking empathy. They want to be seen, heard and acknowledged but the irony is the mere act of complaining is often hard for others to be with. To release complaints, we must acknowledge them first for what they are. They are a request in disguise.

We all like to complain, and venting can be helpful if it's limited. You don't want to suppress your feelings, but you do want to limit the habit of complaining.

When you're venting, you want to be clear with your buddy that's what you're doing. You don't want them to join in or comment, you just want them to witness.

You want to inspire yourself to take empowered action in your life.

1. Take all the complaints that you've been tolerating in your life and list them out below.
2. If it helps you to vent, set a timer and yell, scream and vent them out. If you choose to do this with someone, make sure they know not to collude with your rants – just witness.
3. Have self-compassion and normalise this to yourself: "Of course you feel this way, it's not fair, it is shit."
4. Then take each one in turn and do the mental work to identify the request that sits beneath the complaint.

Complaint e.g. You never tidy the dishes away after you cook

_____

_____

_____

_____

_____

Request e.g. I appreciate when you support me by tidying the dishes away. Please could you help me with this?

_____

_____

_____

_____

_____

Case Study

Build your support team

Angela, late 30s
Full time, Financial Advisor
Self-imposed limitation: "I'm afraid I will fail"
Courage practice needed: Define Your Emotional Support Team

The core issue

> *"I know I want this on some level but if I'm honest I'm scared. What if it's the wrong thing for me?"*

Angela wanted to start her own business. She had an MBA and a sharp mind. Her family had been proud when she had begun her career with an insurance company on a graduate training scheme and had taken a keen interest as she rose through the ranks.

Angela didn't like the bureaucracy which she found herself navigating. The old style of control, authority and micromanagement frustrated her. She had made the decision to start her own business as a financial advisor.

Her family and friends were shocked because to them she was at the height of her career success. Whilst Angela didn't let these opinions sway her, they did put her attention on the negatives of what might go wrong.

Angela had the knowledge and skills to embark on setting up and running her own business and a clear vision of how it might unfold. But she felt emotionally unsupported. She came to coaching describing the feeling metaphorically as being about to jump out of an aeroplane but terrified your parachute won't open and everyone pointing out that danger to you.

This was confusing Angela and had her question her own mind. She knew that she didn't behave like most managers, and she wondered if she was setting herself up to fail. She tried joining start-up groups for entrepreneurs, but she didn't find that environment supportive to her emotional well-being because it tended to be an exchange of business and pitching ideas.

Our work together involved creating a new support team. She had to process the feelings that arose from the comments those who loved her had made and move away from reacting to them into creating proactive and courageous action.

In the first instance, Angela had to rely on my belief in her because she was in a vulnerable and fragile place with her dream. Whenever you put anything out in the world, whether it's a piece of art, a new idea, an opinion, or an application, it's an act of vulnerability because you don't know what's on the other side of that.

It's also an act of claiming your own worth and that can be tough, particularly if you've been your own worst critic for much of your life.

Helping Angela build clarity for her own style of leadership gave her confidence that she could make her vision a reality. Reminding her of her platform of strengths, her plethora of experience and her amazing can-do attitude helped her access her inner resourcefulness.

We created a new support team for her and identified who she would go to and for what. She released the resentment and hurt she felt for those around her that seemed to say the wrong things and realised that it wasn't personal to her.

Their comments didn't mean anything about her; they said more about the other person's world view and belief system. That's the thing about opinion, it is based on someone else's experience and world view. Angela learnt to see and separate what was her own and what was someone else's opinion and belief.

Angela found her own inner authority over her vision, her decisions, and her actions. She stopped waiting for permission from those around her and took her own courageous action.

What Angela learnt

To claim her vision in life, despite her fear that it wasn't achievable. To support her in doing this she recognised that she needed to turn to people who have capacity and skills to emotionally support you. Being clear with her requests and detaching from the potential outcome helped her to self-empower and build courageous optimism around her dream. This resulted in her taking the step to build her own business and to go the distance through the first two years with all their ups and downs.

Courage Practice

Define Your Support Team

Your emotional support team are the people you feel completely safe to be yourself with. They don't fix, rescue, scold or blame you when things go awry or you're having a tough time. They just meet you wherever you are, knowing that you are whole, resourceful and creative. They know this will pass and you will move through it.

Identify your emotional support team, what they do and what they don't do, so that you are clear who you are choosing.

Characteristics

_____

_____

_____

Impact

_____

_____

_____

What they do

_____

_____

_____

What they don't do

_____

_____

_____

Ways to make this work

Build your support team

- Only have those in your circle that have capacity.
- You don't have to make excuses for people and tolerate unsupportive behaviour.
- Be brave. Be you. Lean into those that support you unconditionally.

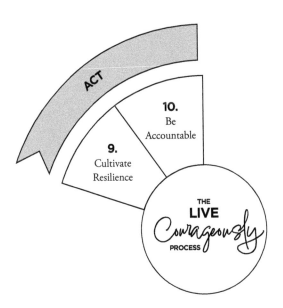

Act

Cultivate resilience

MANAGE YOUR ENERGY SYSTEMS

Cultivating resilience involves the ability to manage your energy to withstand drains and renew it in a way that supports you. It therefore requires you to know that you are innately worthy so that you can create the healthy boundaries needed to enable you to establish limits so that you can focus and conserve your precious energy and attention. Resilience enables you to keep going and see setbacks as temporary whilst continuing the pursuit of your desired vision. So, the Build Personal Resilience courage practice will help you, compassionately and resourcefully, to move through any setbacks.

———————

Resilience is a practice of noticing where your energy is, where it is drained and being able to top it up. It requires you to give yourself permission to stop, check-in and switch things up. Whilst you need a certain level of stress to perform at your best, if you're running on empty you need to prioritise energy recovery and renewal. The opposite is also true – if you're bored and underwhelmed you need to disconnect and reconnect to a different, more positive flow of energy.

At the heart of resilience is the ability to return to a state of inner ease. Stressors are a normal part of your everyday living. It's when you're already full up that you find yourself reacting disproportionately to situations. Accepting that life will throw you lemons, but that you can choose to respond and recover is part of the journey to resilience.

Heartmath™ define resilience as "the capacity to prepare for, recover from and adapt to stress, challenge or adversity".[4] To develop greater resilience, you need to identify strategies to support your recovery from stress.

Think back to Chapter 5 where you considered your natural rhythms. Resilience is linked to that energy management because by focusing on your energy, what restores and depletes it, you can manage your capacity better, stay in positive energy and enhance your productivity.

Reaction is human but when you have awareness, you have choice. When you react unconsciously there is no choice. Highly-charged depleting emotions result in you losing emotional energy. That energy could be used more constructively in supporting you to feel capable, calm and confident to achieve your vision. Resilience enables you to choose, to recover from the energy depletion, and support yourself by doing things that restore and renew your energy.

For full disclosure, I am not a natural 'let go' person. One of my habits is to overthink, to try and get some sense of control. It's that thinking that saves me having to 'feel' it. It doesn't help. The discomfort is always there under the surface.

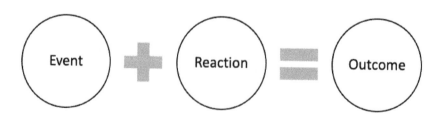

If I apply my old habit to this the equation looks like this:

From this place there is little space for transformation, just a huge amount of wasted energy that creates sluggishness and anxiety.

I have a number of go-to resilience/let go practices: walk the dogs, hug a tree, run, do yoga, b-r-e-a-t-h-e, eat carefully, drink water, be in nature, b-r-e-a-t-h-e some more, remind myself that "this too shall pass", b-r-e-a-t-h-e again. If I apply these, my outcome now looks different.

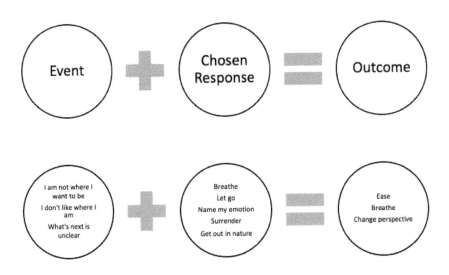

Stuck in what's happened and what's next

When things don't go according to plan, you can get caught between the past and the future and the drama of it all. It's an energy drain where you can't build resilience because you're stuck in the cycle, wasting effort. Sometimes it's a matter of going back to your values to remind yourself what's important. At other times it involves being honest with yourself, accepting where you are caught in drama and taking responsibility for how that's impacting your ability to focus so that you can take positive steps to pivot towards what you want.

The following questions can help you to find focus and decide where to direct your attention when you're stuck:

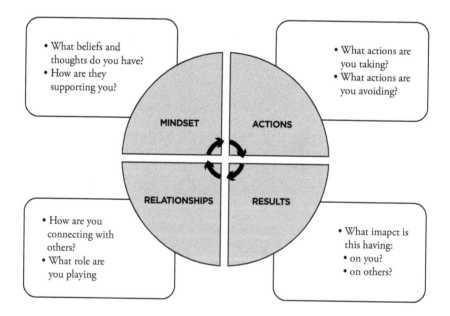

- What beliefs and thoughts do you have?
- How are they supporting you?

- What actions are you taking?
- What actions are you avoiding?

MINDSET

ACTIONS

RELATIONSHIPS

RESULTS

- How are you connecting with others?
- What role are you playing

- What imapct is this having:
  - on you?
  - on others?

Name your resilience strategies

Resilience is not just about the ability to bounce back from setbacks. It's also about being in the process as it's happening and then being able to recover, restore and renew your energy. There will be times when you go down the metaphorical tube but just like when you hold your breath, there will be a bounce-back and you will come up the other side. Still, it's those moments of being in the thick of the hard stuff that you can find incredibly challenging.

Your medicine is inside you. You know what helps you get through and thinking about it and defining your medicine in each area will give you the opportunity to bring that into conscious awareness, rather than grasping for anything to make you feel better when you're at a low ebb.

Knowing what situations renew your energy gives you the chance to choose them, particularly when your resilience is low. It's the same principle as with strengths. When you choose to be with people that lift you or spend time doing an activity that gives you a sense of accomplishment, you feel good. It builds your reserves. Just as if you spend your time holding your breath, feeling anxious, you are going to drain your reserves.

Think through your strategies for topping up your battery. What do they include for each area?

Physical	Mental	Emotional	Spiritual
e.g. walk in nature, breathwork, sleep, mindfulness, laughter	e.g. journaling, thought-stopping, 'body scan', adopting a growth mindset or positive attitude	e.g. talking to support buddy, listening to music, being by water, getting active	e.g. revisiting purpose and values, forest bathing, reading inspirational books or quotes, reminding yourself of positive feedback

So, now define your own resilience strategies:

Physical

_____

_____

Mental

_____

_____

Emotional

_____

_____

Spiritual

_____

_____

Emotions can drain your resilience

The emotional domain is the area where you are likely to experience most energy drains. You're human and you will get triggered emotionally but when you are present to what's going on you have that choice that I mentioned in Chapter 7.

Think about some of the questions you ask yourself during a difficult emotion. I will wager the comments and questions aren't always constructive in moving you forward.

Clients typically describe asking questions like:

- Is it just me?
- Will I ever get over this?
- What if I never meet someone like this?
- What if I got it wrong?
- What if the next thing isn't any better?
- Why is this so hard?
- Why does this hurt so much?
- What if something bad happens?

These questions don't support their resilience because they come from a place of fear and anxiety. When you act from fear or anxiety you seek to control. What you need to do is turn to your soothing strategies and find your medicine within. You need to acknowledge and witness your feelings as valid, and reassure yourself that this too shall pass.

It's easy in these difficult moments to slide into catastrophising. It's hard to imagine better days when your heart is sore. But the narrative that you make up in these moments matters. If you choose a narrative that asks questions that undermine your resilience, you will increase your anxiety and create more doubt.

Watch out for over-caring

Women are known to be nurturers, but empathy is a strength that like any other can be overused. When you find yourself lost in the emotion of it all, you are likely to have fallen into over-caring or, as Kim Scott describes in her book *Radical Candour*, 'ruinous empathy'.[5]

To become conscious with your care requires you to balance your head and heart. You need to trust in others' innate resourcefulness to resolve their own challenges and trust that they can align their own authentic choices and actions. Check whether you are falling into over-care by enquiring whether you are unintentionally disempowering someone by attempting to rescue them. You are responsible for holding your own emotional boundaries; you do not have to soak up others' emotions like a sponge.

Manage your triggered self

Part of your emotional resilience requires you to know when you're triggered. People will say and do things that seem to automatically hook you. Suddenly you find yourself in an exchange that was never your intention to participate in, but you're caught up, overwhelmed by emotions and unable to respond in a way that you would like – none of this is serving you.

The key is to be able to get to a point where you can notice, choose not to react, and explore what is arising in you because of being in relationship with the other person.

When you are aware of what triggers you, it will help you to retain your resourcefulness. It's not only how you respond in the moment but it's also how you think about that reaction afterwards that influences your recovery. Self-criticism and judgment will keep you stuck in a reactive self-limiting cycle. Instead, choose curiosity to learn what got triggered and do the inner work to resolve it.

Part of this process involves teaching people how to treat you when you're triggered. They will know from their own experience that when they're triggered the outcome of a conversation is not good. Where possible, have conversations that think these things through in advance so that you can agree how to navigate those moments.

Reflection: identifying your triggers

I invite you to identify situations that bring out your triggered self. Spend some time journaling on the following questions:

- What situations or experiences trigger you?
- What do those situations have in common?
- What limiting beliefs get triggered in you?

Having identified what triggers you, now reflect on what you need in those situations to get some distance and perspective. Remember, when you're triggered, it's just a part of you that wants to protect you (albeit unskillfully). If you can slow down, you can then notice the emotional reaction and can choose to feel that emotion and not act it out.

By acknowledging the upset (to yourself) of triggered situations, you can choose how you respond. This in turn stops triggered emotions from draining your energy and resilience and enables you to focus your energies more productively. Now, isn't that more positive for you and for those around you?

Disempowerment vs empowerment

What is self-empowerment? I believe it involves knowing your power and allowing it to flow through you without stemming that flow. I've explored self-empowerment in many different ways. I've researched it, I've tried to encourage it in the organisations I've worked in, I've written about it and yet, when I step back from it, I think it's simple.

It's about feeling your power, embracing it, and letting it out.

There are all sorts of ways you can disempower yourself with sabotaging voices. You know from the previous chapters that it's important to manage those internal, fear-driven voices. Yet how do you empower yourself when you feel like you're losing power?

There are loads of tips and tricks that people will tell you help, and I think the biggest one for me is about detaching from the outcome. Holding on to a vision of how it all should be, whilst you're experiencing the toughness of life, is hard.

I believe that, when you hold on to these preordained outcomes that you've selected, it gives you some of your biggest challenges. Because, at the end of the day, you're still trying to control everything instead of creating a flow.

I'm reminded of Gaudi and the Sagrada Familia in Barcelona. He knew that the construction would last for centuries, and that he would never see its completion in his lifetime. He focused on the front of the cathedral so that the generation which began this work would experience a form of completion. The works began. The first stone was laid over 130 years ago and it is scheduled for completion in 2026 (the 100th anniversary of his death).

It seems incredible to me that this Catalan architect could hold a vision of such magnificence and trust in its completion a century after his death. It's such an incredible offering to society, that you can dream small and large dreams to put your creativity or expression in the world and let go of needing to experience the reality of them. After all, nothing is certain in life.

I know in writing this book I have had many starts, stops and stalls. As soon as I make it about the end game, I hit walls quickly and it feels like hard work. It's not that I don't want my work to be successful and help others, it's more that now I realise I do my best work when I'm loving what I do and letting go of the need to have it be a success.

Guilt and shame

Feeling guilt that you're not doing enough
Feeling selfish or guilty for putting your needs first
Going against the selflessness and conditioning that was modelled by the previous generation
Feeling you don't deserve to slow down
Feeling self-care is indulgent
Worried about saying "No" to people
Concerned about being seen as selfish for holding boundaries

These were some of the themes from the survey and are consistent with my experience of coaching women. Women feel guilty if they want to spend some time on themselves, they feel guilty if they invest in themselves, they feel guilty if they say no to someone that needs help, they feel guilty that they have a happy life when someone else is suffering, they feel guilty about the inequity in the world.

Guilt is not shame. The critical difference between them is that guilt is a negative valuation of your behaviour whereas shame is a negative valuation of yourself. I did something bad vs I am bad.

Guilt doesn't affect your core identity of who you know yourself to be. You might feel regret and remorse, but it doesn't mean anything about you personally. Shame on the other hand affects you deeply because it is associated with feelings of inadequacy or unworthiness.

Brené Brown defines shame as "the intense painful feeling or experience of believing we are flawed and therefore unworthy of acceptance and belonging".[6] Shaming by others may be explicit, through comments such as

"If you want to lose weight you might try exercising a bit more", or implicit through non-verbal behaviours like eye-rolling, sarcasm and belittling.

When you shame someone, you puff up your ego by creating a sense of superiority. When you shame yourself, you are at war with the different parts of you. If you have a habit of shaming, you will be well-practised at turning against yourself and personalising failure. Rather than something unfortunate or bad happening, you will personalise it in some way.

Becoming conscious of the language patterns you're using with yourself will help you to identify whether you're using shame unconsciously. Empathy is the antidote to shame. If you want to build resilience you need to turn towards mistakes with love and compassion, not with judgement and shame. And if you habitually go to shame yourself, it's an area where you may wish to prioritise acting differently towards yourself.

Guilt and shame were two of the emotions that I experienced as I navigated my divorce and beyond. I felt shame that I had done something bad that had caused my husband to feel unable to connect and talk to me. I felt shame that I must be a bad wife and mother who had ended up in a situation where the only way forward was divorce. This guilt was rooted in my core limiting belief that I was somehow defective.

But I also felt guilt over the girls and the fact that I had to live with my parents for 12 months to get myself back on my feet financially and find a new house. I felt guilt that their lives were disrupted. I felt guilt that they would have their own emotional experience on the back of this situation.

I feel very fortunate, though, that I chose not to take those feelings and act them out in vengeful or hating ways. I was able to transcend them but only through the therapeutic work of acknowledging them first.

"I feel guilty" is a phrase I hear so many times in coaching. It's the guilt that blocks progress and movement. Women deal with guilt in many ways. They might share it, block it, or project it onto someone else through blame or by blaming themselves. It has them spinning in all directions, avoiding taking the action they need to manifest their dreams.

Guilt is wrapped up in others' opinions and views of your choices and decisions. It is not rooted in your sovereignty and worthiness.

You have no reason to feel guilty for taking time for yourself, for saying no, for asserting your opinion, for treating yourself, for speaking your truth, for being emotional or for making a mistake. These are all human needs, and you have a right to claim them for yourself.

Saying no or holding a boundary is an act of self-care. As adults we are not responsible for anyone else's actions or their happiness. There is an important distinction between this and people-pleasing, where you can be great at reading others' moods and then accommodate and shape shift to please, when it is expedient to do so. This is about claiming back authority for what you want and what you feel and need, and not changing merely to make others feel more comfortable.

Naming the emotion and using your cognitive awareness to question and challenge these thoughts is a helpful way to move through to what's next. Simply asking yourself if it's true that this is something that deserves a guilty response is a way of helping you get into your logical brain.

Hold accountability with kindness

When you're held accountable for something you say you're going to do, it helps you stay in action and not get knocked off course by your emotions, experiences, or other life events. Finding a way to hold your accountability is part of resilience.

You can hold accountability with kindness. If you hold accountability with shame, it will wipe out your progress and create delays until you feel better.

If you hold your goals with love, kindness and compassion you will make steady progress and be in a better relationship with yourself as you travel.

It's not fluffy. Praise is the most underused tool, and it costs nothing. Finding a way to celebrate the incremental gains will support your longer-term progress.

Beyond expectations

Henry Kimsey-House[7], co-founder of Co-active Coaching, once said to me, "Let go of expectations in favour of abundant expectancy." It has taken me years to fully understand the wisdom in these words.

When you hold an expectation of how fast or slow, how difficult or easy the journey will be, it impacts your resilience to meet what is. If you're someone who holds high expectations for yourself, you're not alone. In my experience there is more of an emotional high and low with expectations than there is with abundant expectancy. Expectations have a fixed nature to them – you either meet them or you don't. By contrast, expectancy has a softer, looser, more hopeful quality.

In the moments of disappointment, asking yourself "What expectation am I holding?" and being prepared to surrender it and allow the bigger, universal unfolding to happen will support you to cultivate resilience.

Develop a practice mindset

One of the things about having a practice mindset is how you see failure. Everything is a learning opportunity and rather than needing to prove yourself, you're always learning, growing and evolving. Failure is therefore a natural part of the process.

Regardless of your relationship to failure, resilience will be gained through practice. How you appraise and evaluate your progress will also be impacted by your mindset.

A practice mindset is one where you acknowledge the ongoing and iterative nature of progress. As you experience setbacks you have the choice as to how you perceive them. If they're all part of the nature of progress, you bring an ease to your performance. You are less likely to catastrophise setbacks and instead turn your attention to looking towards opportunity.

Patience is something that can be cultivated through a practice mindset. It may be that your nature struggles with practice. You might get bored quickly or find consistency and perseverance challenging. You might find routine boring and have a need to keep changing things.

How you are with yourself when you forget or stop your efforts matters. Observe yourself and notice if you chastise yourself for forgetting and choosing not to practise. It's an opportunity to ask yourself which part of you is doing the chastising.

Case Study

Build personal resilience

Pooja, late 40s, married
Full-time, NHS Practice Manager
Self-imposed limitation: "To save time, I'll just do it myself"
Courage practice needed: Stay in Your Own Well of Being

The core issue

*"I feel like I'm carrying everyone's stuff around with me
and I can't seem to stop or change it. It's so unfair."*

Pooja was a practice manager for a group of GP surgeries, who was facing a bit of a crisis with her performance at work and overall feeling of fulfilment.

The working environment was a struggle because it felt like a constant push to just get through the day. The doctors were nice enough, but they were also feeling the strain which made them more irritable and impatient than usual.

They were short on receptionist staff and those that were there were frustrated and complaining about their pay. She was finding it hard to recruit replacements at £9 per hour and the quality of applications was poor. The local supermarket was paying more than they were and the emotional demands of this work were significant because the demand for appointments outstripped the availability of doctors.

Each day felt like the same to Pooja. She would hear the patients', staff and doctors' complaints and feel completely powerless to act. Whilst her home life was good, Pooja's husband was getting fed up with her working late and bringing home her emotional complaints about her day. She felt it just wasn't fair.

Pooja felt her resilience was at an all-time low. She was exhausted by everyone coming to her and not acting on their own initiative. She was overwhelmed from soaking up everyone's emotional responses and trying to problem-solve their issues. She was questioning how long she could continue in this role and how to get herself out of this burnout cycle.

Our work together focused on Pooja re-establishing the rules of engagement with the practice and the team. She began to understand that people coming to her to offload their emotional reactions wasn't healthy or responsible on their part. Furthermore, it didn't help her with her own work and actions.

We talked about resilience and its relationship to energy. We discussed the domains of resilience as if they were buckets of energy: physical, mental, emotional, and spiritual. We explored in turn how much energy she had in each area and what caused them to drop.

Pooja identified that a big part of the problem was that she'd lost sight of why she did this work. The relentless demand had taken its toll and with it her enthusiasm and motivation. It had become a job with little satisfaction or appreciation. She began to reflect on what the team were feeling and identified that this lack of satisfaction and appreciation was systemic.

We talked about the 'Hello my name is' campaign for compassionate care and the profound impact it had left on the NHS. It was started by Dr Kate Granger who was both a doctor and a terminally ill cancer patient.[8] Using social media initially, Kate had encouraged and reminded healthcare staff about the importance of introductions in healthcare. Pooja and I discussed how one person can leave a legacy and explored her initial desire behind becoming a practice manager.

Pooja went back to her values and saw that compassion and integrity were two of her fundamental values. She began to dream about what impact she could have if she stopped losing energy on other people's emotional dramas.

We worked through the drama triangle by Dr Stephen Karpman.[9] It is a dynamic model of social interactions and is made up of 3 archetypal (dysfunctional) personas: the victim, persecutor and rescuer. In certain situations, often where there's a power imbalance or potential conflict, we can subconsciously take on these unhelpful roles.

The persecutor is the critical persona who blames, dominates and criticises. The victim is the persona that feels "poor me" and that things are happening to them. The rescuer is the persona who wants to make things better, fears not being needed, and wants to help others but is avoiding helping themselves. These roles interchange: one minute you can feel like "Poor me, it's so unfair" and the next you're in the persecutor role, "Why didn't you do that when you said you would?"

Once you realise that you're caught in the drama triangle, you have the choice to step out of it by stepping into either a challenger, coach or creator role. In becoming aware that she was in a drama triangle with the doctors and receptionists and that she was falling into the role of rescuer, Pooja was able to take charge and step into a new coach role. She began to develop her coaching skills so that she could begin changing the nature of her conversations with the doctors and colleagues.

This is what is known as the empowerment triangle[10]. Asking yourself what you want can take you out of victim and into the creator role. Stepping out of rescuer role involves choosing to claim the coach role and asking the other person what they need, and trusting in their own resourcefulness to solve their issues. Finally, to claim the challenger role you need to let go of blame and choose assertiveness over aggression.

So, when receptionists came to complain to her, she began to ask them about what they needed and how they felt they could resolve their own issues. She was pleasantly surprised by the number of ideas that came forward from them.

When doctors in the practice came with puppy dog eyes and asked her to do a favour for them by completing their paperwork, she told them what she would have to stop doing to meet their request. They started to see the impact of their requests and instead of just saying yes, she offered to show them how to use the system better to facilitate their needs. Whilst it might have taken longer in the short term, she soon realised the benefits when they stopped interrupting her workflow.

As things improved in the day-to-day activities within the practice, Pooja was able to get into a more creative and strategic mindset. She started to identify small but significant changes that would improve the patients' journey and experience through the practice. This reconnected her to the reason why she had undertaken this role in the first place and her bigger purpose of giving everyone equal access to healthcare provision.

As Pooja fixed the leaks in her resilience buckets, her energy returned and with it her optimism and joy for work and life. She stopped going home complaining and was able to leave work at the practice door when she shut it at night.

What Pooja learnt

Doing for other people what they can do for themselves creates dependency. In learning the skills of listening, asking questions and holding others as capable of finding their own solutions, Pooja was able to push back and empower others. She recognised when she was in victim mode and learnt that to get out of it required her to step into the coach role. This in turn stopped her own feelings of powerlessness and helped her to feel more authentic and honest.

Courage Practice

Build Personal Resilience

We all have lapses in practice; it's human and part of our shared experience. Resilience involves recovery and bounce-back. Avoiding the self-blame and criticism will support you to build your resilience practices.

- Reflect on times when you have felt victimised. Identify the steps that helped you to self-empower
- Decide what resources need to be in your well of being to keep you feeling alive and full of health striving
- Give yourself permission to prioritise that
- Release any guilt and narratives that cause you to deprioritise this

Ways to make this work

Cultivate resilience

- Movement is better than staying stuck.
- If you feel like you've taken an emotional hit and are struggling to bounce back, set a timer and allow yourself to wallow in your feelings for one hour.
- After this time get up and act on something. It doesn't matter how small; just take one step towards something you've been putting off. This will get you in motion and build your resilience.
- Saying "No" takes courage! Practise doing so when this protects your needs.
- And ensure your "No" is a real one, not just one said with a smile to appease, as this undermines its purpose.

Be accountable

ACCOUNTABILITY REINFORCES AUTHENTICITY

Critical to the impetus to act is accountability, and so being accountable is the final element in the courage process. You are much more likely to do what you say if you are accountable, to yourself and to others. In turn, accountability bolsters the power of your support team, as they should be accountable too, along with all the other key players in your professional and personal realms. None of this is about blame – it's about taking responsibility and being clear on where the boundaries lie of what you can influence in any given situation. Accountability and authenticity are linked – each reinforces the other, as the courage practice Be Accountable and Authentic demonstrates.

Being accountable to your values and your principles is of course a fine moral imperative. It is also an excellent way to ensure that you act authentically. If you are acting according to your beliefs, then you cannot act in a way that simply accommodates others. Holding that authentic, accountable line is the ultimate act of courage – as we have seen, there are so many temptations along the way to deviate from this path. This is not about being self-righteous or judgemental – it is simply about holding a line that ensures that, every day, you can look in the mirror and say that you have acted with integrity, consistency and, yes, courage.

All this releases any residue of guilt in wanting to pursue success, in wanting to be clear and determined in focusing, as a woman, on your goals.

Release the need to be liked and approved of

The likeability trap was a theme that was present in several responses to my survey. It's a notion that if you advocate for yourself and make your needs important, people won't like you. It sets you up to hustle for likeability and makes self-expression and assertion challenging because you fear the potential consequence of being rejected in some way.

There are many reasons why being liked seems important and, put simply, it feels good and provides a form of self-protection (if you like me, you won't hurt me) which in turn helps you to feel secure.

You may recognise your own need to be liked through examining your own behaviours:

- Do you say yes when you don't want to?
- Do you over-think decisions and end up procrastinating because you're thinking about things from every angle to avoid upsetting others?
- Do you try to make the right decision for everyone involved?
- Do you have a persistent feeling that you're not good enough, no matter how hard you try?
- Do you have a need for praise yet find it hard to accept?

When you haven't accepted yourself, you look for acceptance from others and that's difficult as a leader, parent or partner because it has you doing things that aren't in line with your truth. It may cause you to shapeshift to fit someone else's energy and needs or yield to someone else's positional power or authority.

Define what success means to you

Post-divorce I got stuck in survival mode, saying yes to every piece of work, afraid I wouldn't have enough to meet my financial commitments. I became increasingly nervous about saying no and the potential impact on the relationship with the companies I worked for.

You can only manifest a dream if your structured belief system supports that possibility. The challenge for me was that my belief system didn't support my vision. My subconscious brought up limiting beliefs when things were hard that caused me to start to doubt my ability to create my vision of financial security.

I would turn to my family and friends for support, but the challenge was that they had their own definitions and limits around success. They wanted me to flourish but they were also bound by their own sets of beliefs. They imparted their wisdom, but it came from their own lived experience. The key was to recognise that this was their truth, not the only truth.

As I've said, I had wanted to write this book for a long time. I'd written blogs for different magazines and published my own, created e-books and had a previous manuscript that I'd lost. I had never been able to make the leap to write a book. I knew I wanted to write it, but I kept stalling. I would find excuses or make up stories as to why I wasn't ready yet.

When a friend and colleague shared her published book with me, I asked her how she'd done it. She said she hired a mentor. I started to tell her how I wished I could afford that, and she looked at me and asked me if I could afford not to. She then told me how she had paid for it in instalments.

At the time I was investing heavily in house improvements. I was terrified to invest in something I didn't know I could do or whether it would succeed. But then I also thought, "I had these feelings of envy towards my friend's achievement, but I too could have what she has if I choose to invest in myself".

I decided to ignore the people around me that acted with shock and surprise when they heard I would be writing a book. I chose not to react to the naysayers around me and trusted my instinct to take the leap. I invested in mentoring and as you can see in reading these words, the rest is history.

Having a mentor helped me to get out of my own way. I was able to declare what I didn't know and get help from someone who'd been there. I could share my fears that my writing wasn't clear, and she took each obstacle and helped me to remove it. She held me accountable and told me when I'd done enough perfecting and it was time to act.

During the process of writing this book I found myself changing, editing and generally shape-shifting. I realised I was unconsciously trying to protect myself from rejection by having myself try and write for everyone. The outcome was the writing felt vanilla and had an energy of trying to prove myself.

I was writing from my limiting belief, not from my vision. I was trying to ensure that everyone who might read it would like the book, and I was doing all of that unconsciously.

I accepted that not everyone would like or benefit from my writing. But the truth was I wasn't writing for everyone. I was writing it for women who needed to break through their limitations and in breaking through my own I could feel comfortable and deeply authentic with my writing.

Define your own success reflection:

- Consider what success means to you.
- How will you know when you have it?
- What is the feeling tone of it?
- Who are you being in those moments of success?

Find your opinion

If you've conditioned yourself to focus on safety, fitting in, being liked and generally being accepted by the tribe, you will have lost confidence in your own opinion. Frequently women reach out to coaching wanting to find their voice, but the weird thing is they express themselves beautifully during the coaching. They share their feelings, their hopes, and woes.

So why would it be that in a one-to-one setting they find it easy to express their opinion but at work or in other relationships something else happens? They lose their voice and their opinion. They hold back. They are worried about what others will think. They fear being rejected. They fear being wrong, ridiculed or shamed.

You may have tried to act your way out of this and project your voice, but the truth is, whilst those skills help, they don't heal the inside wounds that cause you to hide, shrink or quieten your opinion. Your first marriage is with yourself, and it's time to listen and back yourself first. You don't need to fight to be heard. It's about knowing and listening to yourself first. It's about accepting that one of our human needs is to belong and be loved but that doesn't mean you have to change for that to happen. Your job is to be yourself and let others be themselves.

It is not your job to speak for others; they're perfectly capable of doing that for themselves. It is your job to express your own experience. If this is challenging for you, slow down, connect to what you feel and use "I" statements. For example, "I am feeling overpowered by the way you're saying that." "I need you to slow down and give me some time to reflect." "I hear what you're saying and respect your truth but that is different to mine."

Be ok with being the only voice in the room

A common concern amongst women is that they find themselves being the lone voice in the room. Perhaps they identify something and want to express it but find the majority isn't in agreement. Or maybe they notice something in the emotional tone of the meeting that needs saying and they express that, only to find the impact is awkwardness.

When you know yourself, your values and your leadership stake, the next step is to give yourself permission to show up and speak your truth. Being the only voice can be perceived in many ways, but if you use it as evidence to support a limiting belief like you're not smart enough or you're too much, you hold yourself back. Sometimes you will be the only voice in the room and sometimes you won't. Either way your voice matters. If you hold it back it may never get shared, and that wisdom is lost. A significant part of acting with integrity is letting your voice be heard.

Remember Henry Ford's quote, "Whether you think you can or you can't, you're right".[11] It's true. Usually, you will find yourself being correct on the back of speaking up. Your job is to open your voice and speak your truth because only you can. And, in my experience, speaking up often opens the floodgates. Other women in the same meeting will say, "So glad you said that, it was exactly what I was thinking!" And then, at the next meeting, they feel emboldened to speak too.

Act from innate worthiness and positive self-regard

Conflict is one of those things that humans are often uncomfortable with. You value and appreciate harmony and belonging so when there's conflict it's difficult. But when parts of you are in conflict it's complicated because it's coming from inside you. Therefore, it's called self-sabotage. It's during these times that it helps to make a request to yourself to stay open to the experience and not let self-doubt, embarrassment or old shame-wounds take over.

Owning your worth presumes that a part of you knows that you're worthy. There may be a conflict between a part of you that believes you are worthy and a part of you that believes you are not. When you own your worthiness, you can tell people what you think, how you feel, and express that what you feel would be beneficial for them. When you accept your worthiness, you are not open to manipulation and confusion.

If you find yourself getting triggered by others not respecting your boundaries or telling you they can't afford your service or even can't help with the chores, remember that it doesn't mean anything about you. It's an opportunity for you to remind yourself of your worthiness. You don't have to always be the one that does the tidying up. You don't have to subjugate your needs for the rest of the family's. You *do* have to decide that your worthiness is not negotiable. You must decide that you matter and act from this place of alignment and integrity with yourself.

Conflict is neither good nor bad – it's neutral and simply a signal that something wants to unfold. You may be someone who chooses to avoid conflict but if you silence yourself or hold back for the sake of harmony it's inauthentic to the relationship. Get comfortable with conflict and remember that it's not personal. It's a sign that the relationship wants something to change. Be your own truth-teller, know what values you're leaning into and use them as your compass to help you navigate.

Be aware, don't manipulate, don't attack

It might sound obvious but falling into blame, defensiveness, stonewalling and contempt is easy when you're frustrated, afraid or angry. Seeing someone's perspective when you perceive that they're behaving unreasonably is hard but it's something that will help you move beyond toxic behaviours. How often do you find yourself in arguments that feel like you're playing ping-pong back and forth? There are no winners because everyone loses in this point-scoring game.

It's in these moments that you need to focus on the goal. What is it that you're trying to achieve? What's important about that? How can you and the other person align around that goal? Whether it's cleaning up your room or delivering on a sale, what's important for both of you and how can you achieve that together?

A coaching colleague of mine shared a wonderful story about her son. She was going through a hard time with her divorce, and she really needed support, but her 11-year-old son just didn't want to tidy up his room. After nagging, cajoling and asking didn't work she realised her approach wasn't working and was creating more friction and upset than helpful progress.

She reflected on what was important about this and what experience she wanted to have with her son. She wanted more fun and joy in their lives and yes, she still wanted the place tidy. She sat down and had a talk with him and asked what way they could get the tidying done but also have fun. Together they came up with a solution which was they would set a timer for 10 minutes each day where they would play loud music whilst they both tidied. The tidying got done but what was more important was that they did it together whilst having much needed play and fun time.

Sometimes you can get so caught up in the outcome of how things need to be that you forget that the way you do it and the how matters. I know for myself that I can be a tyrant boss to myself, making myself graft for 9 hours straight and then sleep and get up and do it all again the next day. But I have learnt that I am most productive when I work with my natural rhythms, in 90-minute bursts. I intersperse my day with dog walks in nature, music, reading and a variety of tasks.

I've got much better at not letting others dictate my day or encroach on it. I've learnt that when friends call and say, "Hey, what are you up to?" what they really want to know is if I'm free to hang out. I used to say, "Nothing much" and then find myself looking for excuses to get off the call. Now I'm honest and I don't answer that question directly. I simply ask them why they're asking.

The bottom line here is your time, resources, opinion, energy and esteem are your business. You are not reliant on others for any of it. Even if you are working a nine-to-five job, you have choices. You may think you have none because your day is structured but you have the choice as to how you meet that day and how you set yourself up for success.

Be conscious of your roles

Part of acting with integrity involves consciously choosing the roles you occupy. Being a leader in your own life means taking ownership of that role as opposed to taking on things because of some sense of obligation or duty.

There may be roles that you don't want to occupy but the situation requires you to. For example, I would prefer not to occupy the role of sales and marketing in my business and that has been the biggest challenge to growing my business and improving it.

Over the years I have invested significantly in my professional competence skills and personal development. I studied emotional intelligence, leadership, systemic coaching, resilience and somatic coaching, transformational breathwork, shamanism and yoga. I loved learning and improving my craft but those weren't the skills that I needed to transform and build my business.

The biggest challenge I had was believing in my own worth and transcending my limiting belief that I wasn't capable of running a thriving coaching business because I had a complete aversion to sales and marketing. I invested in a business coach and various business building programmes, but I would still resist the work of being visible and actively marketing my work.

Doing the inner work in conjunction with my divorce had me take full responsibility for my life and business. I had learnt more about the universal nature of life and how if there was a need then the fulfilment of that need must also exist. But the challenge was applying it. I needed to feel authentic and just knowing that the universe wanted to support me to manifest my dream wasn't sufficient. I was out of integrity with myself and I knew it, and that knowing kept me stuck, spinning my wheels.

The shift came in writing this book and finding the authenticity and purpose behind why I am doing all of this. I have told you before about how many people I have had supporting me through this process. But the most surprising ones have been my ex-clients and people in my community.

When I finally gave myself permission to reach out and ask them what they thought, what worked, what didn't and what they would most appreciate, I was able to be in a new relationship with them and my work. I was reminded how having me to support them in their journey was pivotal because it provided a safe space for them to talk about things in a way they never did with anyone else, to share their hopes and fears, to try things out, to fail, to recover and to learn.

I began to fully appreciate my value in walking with them on their own path to finding their authenticity and courage. I found myself letting go of the need to prove myself and be an expert and realised that my true value was in the space I held for them, the belief, the listening, the challenging and loving them wherever they were in their journey.

As women we hold many roles. We may become a wife, partner, mother, employee, business owner, cleaner, cook, organiser etc. We also have inner roles that we adopt: nurturer, rescuer, provocateur, defender etc. When we're unaware of these roles we don't occupy them consciously. We do them because they're what's expected of us.

I realised the role of leader in my life and business involved me being congruent with who I am, what I believe in and what I long to see happen in the women I serve. It was simple: I wanted to help women find their courage, just as I was finding my own.

In my survey responses there were several comments that mentioned an absence of choice. Examples included things like they were looking after parents or children, struggling with deadlines, dealing with others, managing their own energy levels and time, or being run by guilt. These all have an energy of scarcity to them.

I recognised that scarcity energy in myself. My business couldn't grow because I felt I couldn't give it the time and marketing it needed because I had to pay the bills with self-employed associate work (working for another small business as an associate). Unconsciously I had recreated an employment situation whilst being under the label of being self-employed. I had made my business a job and myself a slave to it.

When a business has a name like mine has, 'Courage Unfolding', as the owner I found myself confronted by the need to step beyond my scarcity fears and remember my own courage.

Viktor Frankl wrote in his book *Man's Search for Meaning*, about his experience in a concentration camp.[12] He said, "Everything can be taken from a man but one thing: the last of the human freedoms – to choose one's attitude in any given set of circumstances, to choose one's own way."

He reminds us that even though we are all subject to circumstances in our life we all have the freedom to choose how we will think and respond to them. Examining your thoughts, feelings and choices is an act of courage because it means you are in the centre of your experience. Only you are responsible for how you think and respond.

Courage is not something you either have or don't. It's something that you nurture and grow, and being in integrity with yourself (doing what you say you'll do) supports you to step forward towards your authentic vision and dreaming. Ultimately, it's a choice to take the actions that align with what you say you want or don't. I chose to get clear about what kind of associate work I wanted and how much I could take on whilst leaving sufficient space and time for me to work on my own business.

If you are carrying limiting beliefs, which most of us are, you have the freedom to change those but it requires work to create new neural pathways in your brain to respond differently. The practices in this book will support you to change and rewire some of your thinking and emotional habits of responding, but at the end of the day it comes down to a decision to act with integrity towards yourself and your highest potential.

Identify how you self-soothe

When you don't want to experience emotions, you may find yourself reaching for different numbing strategies. These might include distraction with busyness, shopping, focusing on others or emotionally numbing with food, alcohol etc. This doesn't make the feelings go away – they're still there under the surface and will resurface at the most unexpected of times.

Once you know what helps you soothe yourself, you have a choice to lean into those strategies that will resource you. Examples might be an uplifting playlist, a warm bath, aromatherapy oils, a cosy blanket. Become conscious of what's in your toolkit that helps you feel safe inside so that instead of getting caught in procrastination and distraction you consciously choose what you know supports you to recover your energy and aliveness.

Do what you say you're going to do

When your beliefs, thoughts, emotions and behaviours are in alignment you have integrity and as Don Miguel Ruiz says, "impeccability" with your word.[13] The courage audit in Chapter 3 had you take a deep dive into your beliefs and behaviours and was the start of exploring your overwhelm and stuckness from different levels of perception. But there have been many points in this book where I have raised the issue of integrity and accountability. This isn't about beating yourself up, but it *is* about noticing where something is out of alignment and giving you the invitation to bring that back into focus so that you can create the life and work you want.

At the end of a coaching conversation a natural conclusion is to move towards accountability. Questions are asked like, "How will you hold that accountability for yourself?" The next question from the coach would be, "And how will I (as your coach) know?" which directs the client towards their own agreements with themselves.

Whether you are working with a coach or not, accountability is key, but it's not about someone else always needing to hold accountability for you. It's about holding yourself accountable to the life and work that you want and navigating yourself through the fear zone on your journey.

Accountability reflection

I invite you to explore your relationship with accountability. Are you someone that overcommits, or do you avoid being tied down to a commitment?

- Spend some time in reflection looking back over your relationship to accountability.
- What word describes your relationship to accountability?
- How would you like it to be?
- What do you need moving forward?

Case Study

Take action

Joanne, mid 40s, married, two children
Full-time, Head of Sales
Self-imposed limitation: "I need to be liked"
Courage practice needed: Being authentic and accountable

The core issue

"I just want the team to be happy and get on with things. Why can't people just grow up, work together and get the job done?"

Joanne was head of sales within a technology organisation. She had a busy home life co-parenting her two children with her life partner. She was relatively new into the organisation and this role was a step up for her.

She had felt confident about meeting the ambitious company targets, but the pandemic had made it hard to get out and connect with customers and she had noticed a sharp decline in the team's sales over the past year.

As someone new into the department she had inherited her team of field sales. As part of her approach to galvanising and motivating the team, she decided to call them together for a strategy day.

Her vision for the day was that it would be fun and engaging and focused on delivery, but the reality was different. There were clearly tensions in the team and she could sense conflict. Joanne did her best to explain why the targets had been set in the way they had and to bring hope and clarity to the vision but there were many instances of non-verbal behaviours, sighing and rolling of eyes, that caused her concern. How would they meet these targets when they couldn't get out of the starting blocks?

Joanne felt her confidence levels start to drop, particularly after the series of one-to-one interviews she held with the team. She learnt that they were deeply frustrated over how targets had been set historically, about feeling unheard, and were complaining about each other's behaviours. What had seemed like a clear and achievable brief now seemed murky and less doable.

Furthermore, there were some real concerns about the target audience and their potential investment funds. The car industry was one of their key customers and the chip crisis had meant a pause in investment. Whilst Joanne knew their product and service were excellent, she sensed fear in the team.

Joanne wasn't new to turning around situations but that was when she had been relying on her own strengths of delivery. This was her first team management role, and she needed the team to feel happy and engaged, particularly as each month there was a measurement of engagement (questions about how motivated and supported people felt at work) that each team reported on. Her team's results were showing in the bottom quartile for performance, and she couldn't ignore that. She wanted the team to get along and do great work together but to start with, this meant she focused too much on placating them to gain their cooperation.

At home, life was pressured. The pandemic had meant home schooling and whilst she and her partner had tried to share the load, she knew her teenage son had taken his foot significantly off the gas. The result was that his predicted GCSE grades were low and she felt powerless to motivate him. He was more interested in playing online games with his friends than he was in learning and regurgitating what he saw as useless information.

As part of her induction Joanne worked with me as her coach. She shared with me her concern that she had taken on more than she could handle and her fear that unless she could get the team on board she'd fail in this position.

Joanne had to decide what to address first, and she wanted to focus on her team and her role with them. Her challenge was that she needed to demonstrate improvement in the team's sales performance and to do that they had to stop complaining and procrastinating and focus to deliver results.

She expressed how she was worried about her impact if she went in too hard. She wanted them to like her and to report positively on the engagement touchpoint and she was conscious that this was making her hold back her opinion. She was aware that she wasn't taking action to move forward, and it felt like she was spending too much time listening, reflecting and procrastinating, and not doing anything practical with that information.

We started by focusing Joanne on exactly what she wanted her team to do – concentrate on their sphere of influence. She listed out all the things she was worried about and then she went through them and identified which ones she could influence. Quickly Joanne saw that despite wanting the team to feel good and appreciate her leadership style, worrying about how she came across was going to make her cautious and hypervigilant. She wasn't leading them; she was pacifying them and placing the pressure of their sales targets onto herself.

When I asked Joanne if this need to be liked and appease was familiar, she recalled that growing up she had been repeatedly told that if she didn't have anything nice to say it was better to say nothing at all. Being nice was considered important to success and belonging.

The consequence from this was that Joanne had learnt to focus her energy on being likeable and amenable. She had learnt that it was better sometimes to keep quiet and comply than it was to ask for what she wanted, even if she felt resentful in the long run. Joanne did not see that she had the right to ask her team cleanly and clearly for what she needed. Instead, she was placating them and holding back on her authentic leadership.

Joanne knew that she had to rely on her leadership impact and not her past success in delivering results. She spent time thinking about the individual and collective goals for the team. She thought through what was negotiable and what wasn't. She clearly defined the targets, and the consequences for not achieving them. Next, she identified the behaviours that she wanted to see in the team and set herself targets to acknowledge when these were demonstrated.

Then she had to ask herself who she needed to be as their leader to help this team deliver on this ambition. Joanne learnt that approval-seeking and appeasement was a defensive strategy that she used to protect herself from being seen as not nice and rejected.

What Joanne learnt

She gave herself permission to rewrite the belief that she needed to be nice and replaced it with the need to be authentic. In turn she refocused her own accountability, away from trying to achieve the team's sales targets, and towards that of being the team's leader. When team members complained she asked them to stop and instead make clear requests, not simply complaints and demands. She didn't indulge them with gossip or an acceptance of excuses, and instead asked them what they needed to help them achieve their targets and how they were going to make that happen.

She realised that for her to have boundaries and hold accountability with the team she needed to trust in her own strengths, abilities and professionalism. She changed her style of communication with the team and focused more on clarity and demonstrating leadership. She redefined the boundaries of her accountability and that of her team. This resulted in more direct and honest conversations that in turn led to changes within the team. Some found this new pressure too much and chose to move on and leave the organisation. However, the key members of the team committed to this new way of working, thrived on the challenge and began to deliver improved results.

Joanne now focuses on her leadership of the team and has released herself from the role of getting clients over the line. She uses praise to acknowledge and motivate the team and she has learnt to celebrate herself, not against her likeability, but according to her leadership vision and authenticity.

Courage Practice

Be Accountable and Authentic

Giving yourself permission to speak up for what you need, making clear requests and holding your own boundaries and accountability is a pre-requisite to being a successful leader in your work and in life.

When humans complain to each other, it can quickly become gossip. It's a way of alleviating unwanted emotion and can quickly turn toxic. Chronic complainers and people-pleasing leaders end up in a debilitating pattern where no one wins.

As women, many of us have been conditioned to be nice, to subjugate our needs and comply. Part of stepping into our own authority and leadership involves letting go of these protecting and complying behaviours, expressing our opinion, speaking truth to power and making clear requests. It is a model of adult-to-adult behaviour where others may agree or refuse those requests. You can then choose what to do next, but at that point you are coming from a place of authenticity and authority.

To be accountable requires you to be clear with yourself and others. It takes us right back to the first practice of slowing down and anchoring so that you can listen to yourself and sense what's needed.

Clarity and authenticity are key to accountability. If you are pleasing others, complying and placating, you have given away your authority and are in relationships which are likely to harbour only dissatisfaction and resentment. Becoming your own authority requires you to look in the mirror and ask yourself what you truly desire and then giving yourself permission and accountability to follow that truth.

I don't underestimate the courage needed to be authentic and to be truly accountable. That is why all this is the tenth and final stage of this courage process. However, if you have undertaken the previous stages, of Anchoring, Auditing, Accepting and then Aligning, this Act phase will be the logical next step to take, your reward for the hard work of assessing honestly where you are, and summoning your power as a woman to move forward.

Ways to make this work
Being accountable and authentic

To help to embed these two practices, consider the following every day:

- What is my intention for the day?
- What is the plan for how I will now choose to spend my time?
- Is what I am doing what I authentically want?
- When I do something what will that honour in me?
- How will I hold myself accountable to deliver on my plan?
- How will I come back to the plan when my mood wants to divert my attention?
- What accountability have I agreed with myself and how I am I holding myself to this?
- What accountability have I agreed with others and how am I holding them to this?

Implement the Live Courageously Process

Living fully, on your own terms, according to your rhythm and authority, involves connecting with your courage to overcome doubts, fears and self-imposed limits so that you can make conscious choices and empower yourself.

The more you live and work courageously, the more you will experience authenticity and fulfilment. The less you do it, the more likely you are to suffer the bitterness of regret and resentment. Living courageously is a process with a series of steps to help you identify your authentic truth and claim the life and work that is designed for you. It supports you to accept your doubts but not let them stop you from living and leading your life, your way.

As humans we are all works in progress, constantly learning and growing until our time is eventually up. The Live Courageously Process helps you to coach yourself through the ups and downs of your journey. It is cyclical in nature because life is always evolving and the stressors of today will evolve, and new stressors will arrive. The Process will help you to find your own resourcefulness and build resilience so that you can keep stretching into becoming more of yourself without the strain.

Living courageously is built on a foundation of clarity, conscious choice and intention. In reading this book you have already embarked on your own live courageously process. Let's revisit it here.

Anchor – focus on the here and now & draw on your inner strengths

When life or work is challenging, and you've lost perspective and forgotten your resourcefulness, start the process.

Stop
- constant what-if thinking and rumination.
- casting yourself as the victim asking why this is happening to you, feeling the unfairness of everything, asking what's wrong with you or why you seem to be the only one.
- thinking habitual limiting beliefs that you're not enough as you are.

Anchor
- Focus on your breath and the present moment.
- Remember that you are innately worthy.
- Recall who you are in your strength and at your best.
- Direct your brain to look for evidence of your strength and innate worthiness. This in turn supports you to feel more confident and optimistic.

Audit – simplify your focus & decide what truly matters

When everything is cluttered and there are competing demands, you tend to focus on who shouts the loudest rather than what really matters.

Stop
- reacting to everything and everyone.
- pushing forward hoping you will get on top of everything.
- juggling and switching your attention constantly.

Audit
- Take stock and complete the courage audit.
- Change your perspective and see the bigger picture of your leadership of your life.
- Reconnect with your values and ruthlessly prioritise these so that you can create integrity within yourself.

Accept – build a healthy routine & embrace your own authority

When you feel the pressure to be always 'on' and react quickly or feel the need to please and fit in.

Stop
- reacting to others' agendas and trying to make everyone else happy.
- listening to your inner critic.
- marginalising your wiser, inner knowing.

Accept
- Your first marriage is to yourself – make it a happy one by focusing on your resourcefulness.
- You choose your own rhythm – set it up each day according to your own energy system.
- You have inner authority – exercise it.

The critical importance of embracing our own authority

I am departing from the summary format here to focus specifically on the importance of having your own authority, as this is so critical to the whole Live Courageously Process.

So many women I encounter in my coaching, many of whom are summarised in the featured case studies, tell me how they feel conditioned to think that if they are good or nice, then they will be worthy of love and of achieving success etc. This becomes a condition in place before any of those things can be gained. It is of course, an insidious and false assumption that so often holds women back from being true to themselves, and to others.

The key to living courageously is to become a creator in our lives. To know what we need, what we want, what we value and, above all, to have healthy self-respect. We all need to believe that all this is possible and set the boundaries to claim it for ourselves.

Gaining healthy self-respect requires us to no longer be willing to be emotionally blackmailed or guilted into doing things. We know what we want, and we are willing to back that up with our actions even in the face of others' reactions to this boundary setting. We let go of being in the drama and reacting with them and instead choose to stay focused on what we need to do to thrive.

We stop trying to change other people to make us feel happier. Instead, we focus on ourselves, our values, needs and dreams. This is now not a selfish impulse. We establish the support we need to stay on our path and take the action and accountability to move forward in the direction we have chosen.

In all this, one of the things we let go of is the idea that things are personal when people don't respond in the way we feel they should. Instead, we now have the self-worth to know that we are innately worthy. Of course, along the way we will have successes and failures, but a crucial change is that now we can recognise that these no longer define who we are. For example, if a partner says they don't want a committed relationship, accept that, decide what you want and make your own choices. Don't set about trying to change their mind or cajole or manipulate them, just respect their choices and make your own. In this way you are your own authority.

Align – reimagine your dreams & build your support team

When you're stuck or have lost faith and hope, the mere fact of dreaming can be a struggle.

Stop
- imagining a low dream of the worst possible outcome.
- looking for evidence of why you can't have what you dare to dream.
- being cynical and critical.

Align
- Give yourself permission to dream.
- Discover your best way to dream and imagine a high dream or best possible outcome.
- Find people around you that support you and your dreaming unconditionally.

Act – cultivate resilience and be accountable

This is the moment that brings everything together. After anchoring, auditing, accepting, and aligning, the whole process only takes on meaning in our lives if we act. But to do so is the ultimate act of courage. And so, we need to be tough and resilient. We should recognise that stressors won't go away but we can get better at noticing them, slowing down, pausing and then choosing how we respond. That is resilience in its true practical form.

And then, to see things through, we need to be accountable to others and most importantly, to ourselves. Face things with honesty, through the true self we have discovered by looking in that mirror. In that way, when at the edge of the comfort zone, we won't be afraid to take the next step towards a new way.

Stop
- over-thinking and hesitating
- rehearsing everything in your head
- beating yourself up

Act
- Develop the resilience you need to help you towards action
- Through declared accountability, make it essential that you act
- Start to take the steps you need

Your live courageously process

I cannot stress how much this is a practice – to set your life up by design instead of conditioning or others' expectations.

This practice is designed to help you to overcome successfully the most common issues I am confronted with by women trying to take more control of their professional lives. In my experience these are:

- That feeling of overwhelm from taking on too much of the emotional stuff going on within their teams.
- Trying, all the time as a manager, to please everyone or find harmony and consensus.
- Burnout from not staying focused within the strategic arena and ruthlessly prioritising.
- Falling into the trap of not empowering others and delegating. Instead, getting caught in the drama that plays out in organisations

where, as a manager, you become the part of the problem by trying to fix or rescue everything.

- Grappling with how to deal with team members who display toxic behaviours.
- Struggling to claim a distinctive leadership signature and authority and properly own a seat at the table and being unafraid to express a clear opinion.
- Overcoming the dreaded imposter syndrome when you reach the edge of your comfort zone and avoiding self-sabotaging behaviours.

We have covered these scenarios in various ways in the book, through challenging observations and the case studies. These remain stubbornly common issues faced by people (but, depressingly, overwhelmingly more by women) but, as I have shown, they can and should be overcome. This book is designed to help in that journey. It is all about mindset, emotions and actions.

The Live Courageously Practices have been written for you to discover your authentic self, build a trusting relationship with her and to choose consciously to lead according to who she is. Your work is to find your power and to keep remembering who you are.

- To **anchor** in the present moment and remember your innate strengths and worthiness.
- To **audit** and weed out the clutter of your mind, conditioning, and fears.
- To **accept** your divinity and complexity within you.
- To **align** with your grace, your dreams and what matters to you.
- To **act**, despite the fears, through being your authentic self, and keep walking your path.

The key to all this is developing all those vital views of the self: self-respect, self-worth, self-acceptance, and self-belief. None of these practices can happen without those being in place. By achieving those we can all live courageously by acknowledging our humanity and believing in our innate worthiness.

Interactivity summary

Here's a summary of all the interactive moments in this book.

Exercise	Page	Completed
Breath practice	p.56	
My personal balance sheet	p.59	
Build core strength	p.69	
Courage audit	p.81	
Courage wheel	p.88	
Values mining exercise	p.102	
Healthy vs unhealthy striving habits	p.119	
Habits that nourish / drain	p.126	
Set your own rhythm	p.132	
Meet your inner authority	p.142	
Rule your world reflection	p.153	
Dreaming for logical thinkers	p.163	
Dreaming for creative thinkers	p.164	

Exercise	Page	Completed
Define characteristics of people who you feel safe with	p.179	
Define your red flags in relationship	p.180	
Requests vs. Complaints exercise	p.182	
Define your emotional support team	p.187	
Identify your resilience strategies	p.196	
Identify your triggers	p.199	
Cultivate resilience reflection	p.210	
Define your terms for success	p.214	
Accountability reflection	p.223	
Being accountable and authentic courage practice	p.229	

Next steps

If you've not yet written anything in this book, that of course is fine. However, now that you have read about the whole Live Courageously Process, you have probably reached one of two conclusions. One, that you are already living courageously, and this book has validated your approach to life, work and relationships. If this is the case, then great, spending time and thought on further analysis through the interactive sections of the book may not serve you further.

However, the alternative conclusion might be that the issues raised have resonated with you and you wish to embark (or continue) with the process. If you fall into that category, then I encourage you to do two (or maybe even three) things:

Revisit the interactive responses you have given (or, if you've not undertaken those yet, do so now)

Recognise that this is the beginning, not the end of the journey, and think about the year ahead as one where you will use this book as a companion and a guide. And to that end, I have included a further blank-columned version of the Courage Audit on p.245 for completion one year from now. Why not diarise that date now? And then compare the version you completed on pages 75-80 with the one in a year's time and see the progress you have made.

Work with a coach

This is the third thing for you to consider. My own experiences in working towards a life of courageous living has been, as I have outlined, often faltering and uncertain, and it has taken me some years to arrive at a clear path that works for me, and, as I have now discovered, for many others too. It is therefore a process that benefits hugely from the support and guidance of a companion, a coach along the way. Now, that coach could be anyone you know and trust to help you, but it could also be... me.

I would love to be given the opportunity to talk to you about living courageously, and my contact information is shown below.

If you'd like to be like Joanne, Priya and the other ladies in this book and would value some additional support, you can find out more about how I can help you at http://www.courageunfolding.com.

Sign up for my free resources, attend one of my programmes, or schedule a strategy call with me to discuss how we can work together to bring Live Courageously Processes alive in you, your life and your work.

Go to the website or email me at vanessa@courageunfolding.com.

Handy guide to the Courage Practices

No.	Courage Practice	Page
1.	Slow Down, Pause and Breathe	p.55
2.	Build Core Strength	p.69
3.	Be Intentional	p.93
4.	Live Your Values	p.108
5.	Set Your Own Rhythm	p.132
6.	Rule Your World	p.153
7.	Dare to Dream	p.172
8.	Define Your Support Team	p.187

Follow-up Courage Audit

If you completed the courage audit on pages 82-87 at the time of first reading this book, then it is good to check in on progress you have made since then.

This follow-up courage audit is designed to be used, say, one year on from when the original one was completed. In the intervening period you may have put into practice parts of the process outlined in this book. On that basis, I would hope you have been able to make progress! You can check this by now scoring yourself again, with hopefully a higher number of these points gaining ticks in the 'Always' and 'Sometimes' columns.

	Always	Sometimes	Never
Opinion beliefs:			
My opinion matters			
My knowledge, skills and experience have value			
My feelings count			
My needs and requests are important			
Opinion behaviours:			
I communicate what I see, sense and feel			
I raise concerns			
I ask for what I need			
I make clear requests			
Authority beliefs:			
I am my own best authority			
I trust my intuition			
I am equal in my work relationships regardless of status and power			
I make my own choices			

	Always	Sometimes	Never
Authority behaviours:			
I empower myself and make decisions			
I navigate through fear and doubt			
I stand my ground with strong personalities			
I have self-respect and authenticity			
Personal growth beliefs:			
I am always learning and growing			
There is no failure, only failing to try			
Growth is possible in everything			
The only person I can change is myself			
Personal growth behaviours:			
I set myself goals for what I want to achieve			
I focus on growing my skills and competencies			
I recognise and walk through my learning edges			
I challenge and support myself in equal measures			

	Always	Sometimes	Never
Emotional mastery beliefs:			
All of my emotions are valid			
My emotions deliver information to me			
My emotions are neither good nor bad			
I can master my emotions			
Emotional mastery behaviours:			
I name my emotions			
I process my emotions without defaulting to analysis			
I explore the wisdom my emotions give me			
I can change my emotional state			
Worthiness beliefs:			
I define what success means to me			
I am enough as I am			
I have unique strengths			
I am innately worthy			

	Always	Sometimes	Never
Worthiness behaviours:			
I prioritise what matters to me in my career and life			
I believe in myself			
I advocate for myself			
I am worthy of career advancement			
Fun and recreation beliefs:			
I am the creator of my own experience			
Fun and joy matter to my life			
I can achieve the right balance for me between work and fun			
I can prioritise enjoyment			
Fun and recreation behaviours:			
I prioritise and schedule fun			
I choose activities that light me up			
I am present and in the moment during recreation activities			
I surround myself with people that lift me			

	Always	Sometimes	Never
Boundary beliefs:			
I am allowed to set my own boundaries and tell people what's ok and what isn't			
It's ok to stand up for my preferences and work-life balance			
I choose who to be in relationship with			
I do not have to carry other people's emotional baggage			
Boundary behaviours:			
I set clear boundaries			
I confront bad behaviour			
I do not tolerate poor excuses or people that invalidate my feelings			
I give what's required (not over-giving)			
Accountability beliefs:			
I create my own outcomes			
I create my own psychological safety			
Trust is an inside job			
I am responsible for my own actions			

	Always	Sometimes	Never
If I'm accountable, I'm more likely to do what I say I will do			
I can only be responsible for what I can influence			
Accountability behaviours:			
I keep my word to myself			
I don't overpromise			
I act decisively			
I do what I say I will do			
I declare my accountability, to myself and to others			
I hold others accountable, where appropriate			
I avoid apportioning blame			
I focus on being responsible for things I can influence and change			

About the author

Vanessa believes that the opportunity for women is to return to their wholeness and to reclaim their worthiness from within. She believes that your medicine is inside you and if you slow down, tune in to yourself and build deep inner trust and safety, that magic happens.

At the centre of her work is tuning in to your spirit and allowing it to express itself in the way that only you can. She has often described herself as walking on a continuum between the spiritual and the pragmatic.

She holds an MSc in Organisational Behaviour, MA in Managing Human Resources, is a Certified Professional Co-Active™ coach, Co-Active™v Leadership graduate, Certified Organisation and Relationship Systems coach and Heartmath™ coach. She is also a shamanic practitioner, emotional freedom technique practitioner, qualified yoga teacher and transformational breathworks practitioner.

Vanessa lives in Surrey, UK and works internationally as a leadership coach and consultant. She is a mother of two, sister, and daughter to two parents who have modelled generosity. She is also an owner of a miniature schnauzer called Esther who has shown her the true meaning of being true to your nature and spirit.

Learn more at:
www.courageunfolding.com
www.linkedin.com/in/vanessamay

Bibliography

---

1   Love liberates: Maya Angelou https://www.oprah.com/own-master-class/maya-angelous-master-class-quotes/all

2   Quoted from article on website: Ernest Rossi https://www.ernestrossi.com/interviews/ultradia.htm

3   Caitlin Walker & Marian *Way So you want to be drama free* Clean Publishing. ISBN 978-0-9574866-3-8 p116

4   Heartmath Coach Training & Certification Programme c2015. Institute of Heartmath 14700 West Park Avenue, Boulder Creek, California, 95006

5   Kim Scott *Radical Candor: How to get what you want by saying what you mean xii* Preface St Martin's Press 14 Mar. 2017

6   Brené Brown *Atlas of the Heart* Penguin Random House c 2021 p137

7   Henry Kimsey-House, CoFounder, Former Co-President Co-active Training Institute

8   Dr Kate Granger https://www.hellomynameis.org.uk/

9   Dr Stephen Karpman https://karpmandramatriangle.com/ and the empowerment triangle https://theempowermentdynamic.com/individuals/

10   https://theempowermentdynamic.com/about/

11   Henry Ford *My Life and Work* Phoenix Classics, Ebooks, 26 Sept 2021

12   Viktor E Frankl *Man's Search for Meaning* June 1 2006, Beacon Press, ISBN 9780807014295 (ISBN10: 080701429X)

13   Don Miguel Ruiz *The Four Agreements* Amber-Allen Publishing 10 July 2018, ISBN-10 9781878424310. Pg. 25

Ingram Content Group UK Ltd.
Milton Keynes UK
UKHW020227010423
419458UK00006B/45